TEXAS GHOSTS

HOUSTON, GALVESTON, AND VICINITY

OLYVE HALLMARK ABBOTT

Schiffer
Publishing Ltd®

4880 Lower Valley Road, Atglen, Pennsylvania 19310

Copyright © 2010 by Olyve Hallmark Abbott
Library of Congress Control Number:
2009936776

Designed by "Sue"
Type set in Demon Night/New Baskerville BT

ISBN: 978-0-7643-3410-8

Printed in The United States of America

Schiffer Books are available at special
discounts for bulk purchases for sales
promotions or premiums. Special editions,
including personalized covers, corporate
imprints, and excerpts can be created in
large quantities for special needs. For more
information contact the publisher:

Published by Schiffer Publishing Ltd.
4880 Lower Valley Road
Atglen, PA 19310
Phone: (610) 593-1777; Fax: (610) 593-2002
E-mail: Info@schifferbooks.com

For the largest selection of fine reference
books on this and related subjects, please visit
our web site at **www.schifferbooks.com**
We are always looking for people to write
books on new and related subjects. If you have
an idea for a book please contact us at the
above address.

This book may be purchased from the
publisher. Include $5.00 for shipping.
Please try your bookstore first.
You may write for a free catalog.

In Europe, Schiffer books are distributed by
Bushwood Books
6 Marksbury Ave.
Kew Gardens
Surrey TW9 4JF England
Phone: 44 (0) 20 8392-8585;
Fax: 44 (0) 20 8392-9876
E-mail: info@bushwoodbooks.co.uk
Website: www.bushwoodbooks.co.uk

Dedication

To my family, who means everything, and to Robyn Conley, whom I'd like to claim as family.

CONTENTS

Acknowledgments

Stories don't just appear from nowhere, although by many reports, ghosts do. Numerous individuals have given me valuable information in my research. Many of whom I've met, and some I haven't, but all were glad to help add to this book.

My gratitude goes to Dash Beardsley, Dennis Beck, Pete and Carolyn Haviland, Dianne McCartney, Rich Smith, Neal Witwer, Randy Woods and to the Freelance Writers Network. Also, fondest memories of historian, John Allwright, whom I knew too short a time.

Robyn Conley, as always, a friend and mentor.

Thanks to those in the ghost trenches who helped me with my research: Connie, Colleen, Sherri Sinisi, John & Bob Sanders, Kelly & Susan McClain, Nikki Hampton, Sandra McMasters, George and Beth Iberra, Mazen Zeiden, Scott Wells, Jamie Salinis, Carolyn Wengler, Kim Dyer, Linda Rial, Amy Scorazzi, Steve Havlock, Dave & Dinah Olsen, and Barb Gatlin.

To Dinah Roseberry, my super editor at Schiffer Publishing, I give special thanks. She knows about ghosts and all their pseudonyms.

And last, I must acknowledge all the spirits who gave me the inspiration to write this book.

SPECIAL THANKS TO:

DASH BEARDSLEY

Dash founded the original historical Ghost Tours of Galveston Island in 1999. During this two-hour tour, Dash informs members of ghost stories, legends, and the mysteries of the island. He imparts his own fascination of the paranormal to the people he escorts around those special places on this very haunted island. His tour ranked #2 in the nation in 2008 and #1 for 2009.

Check with www.ghosttoursofgalvestonisland.com for information.

PETER JAMES HAVILAND

Pete and his wife, Carolyn, are well-known in "Texas paranormal." Pete has researched paranormal phenomena for over twenty years. He is a certified clinical forensic hypnotherapist; Co-host of Parahub Radio, field investigator for the Office of Paranormal Investigations; Co-founder of Paranormal Research Organization; SE Texas Area Rep for American Ghost Society; Communications Coordinator for AGS; president/lead investigator of Lone Star Paranormal Investigation (www.lonestarspirits.org), and member of the American Association Electronic Voice Phenomena. Pete is called upon for speaking engagements and workshops.

RANDALL L. WOODS

Randall is owner of "Woods and Associates"— Newspaper Publisher, Marketing Services and Public Relations in The Woodlands. The Federal Government has recognized his professional accomplishments, to which there is a long list. He also served as press secretary for President Gerald Ford. During the time he published *The Spring Souvenir* newspaper in Old Town Spring, he occupied the Doering Court "barn." When he realized a little girl haunted the building, he began researching the paranormal and formed "The Walking Ghost and History Tours of Old Town Spring." It has been featured in local and national media and has hosted groups from throughout the United States and Europe. Visit www. oldtownspringonline.com for more information.

RICH SMITH

Rich investigates all phases of the paranormal and is a skilled technical specialist with Electronic Voice Phenomena (EVP). A frequent speaker on the subject throughout the state, he is author of *Everyplace I Go is Haunted*, which includes a CD of recorded voices. Rich also teaches classes in EVP with field trips, computer analysis, and recording technique sessions. While driving along Texas highways, watch for Rich and Mary Smith's motor home painted with their caricatures. You'll know it's Rich and Mary traveling to a paranormal workshop, a speaking engagement, or to seek out a "new" old haunted place. Don't miss his informative and entertaining website at www.paratexas.com.

INTRODUCTION

In planning my research trip to the Texas coastal area, I made my reservations and all but packed my luggage for the first week in September 2008. The thought of visiting all the spirit-occupied places I had heard and read about intrigued me, and I hoped to find many more.

A few days before my departure date, the weather forecast warned of a storm. Since I couldn't very well shoot pictures in the rain, I delayed my trip. Had I followed my earlier plans, I would have been there and gone before Hurricane Ike rocked the Texas coast on September 13. I also couldn't have included results of the immediate aftermath of the 2nd worst flood in Texas history.

I drove to South Texas in October and again in April 2009. Unless we see for ourselves, the impact of a hurricane on people, their homes, businesses, and the land itself, is next to impossible to fathom.

After returning home, I was ready to complete my third ghost book. You may be familiar with a few of these legends, but there is always room for more details in a new, old haunted tale.

I still can't forget the gray figure, about four feet tall, dashing across the hall in the Baker Hotel of Mineral Wells during a midnight investigation with paranormalists, Chris Mosley and Pete Haviland. It wasn't a mouse, and it was bigger than a breadbox. Besides, it wore a hooded cape, like the little creature in the movie, *Don't Look Now*. Chris told me later that I wasn't the only one who had seen the same apparition.

There are those who believe in ghosts and those who are convinced (read pretty sure) there are no such things. But consider the people who haven't quite cast their votes. I would never try to dissuade anyone from a skeptical preference, unless, of course, I could prove ghosts exist, which I can't. It's a work in progress for everyone who has paranormal interests.

The journey in this book takes us into the spectral world, south on Interstate 45, depending on where you begin, all the way to Galveston, with short detours along the way. My first stop was The Woodlands, where

I thought I'd look into "An RX for Murder," at Walgreens. Everyone loves a good ghost story. After checking out the drugstore, my next stop was across Interstate 45 to Old Town Spring.

Absorb the history—read the tales with a clear mind. Decide for yourself if disembodied souls are among us. Most of the pictures in this book are within weeks after Hurricane Ike. Memories of the tragic storm will remain for years to come in the minds of those who live along the coast. It is to them and the families they touch that we offer our hope for the future.

The Woodlands

When the Europeans first arrived in what is now Montgomery County, the Atakapa Indians occupied the area. The Arkokisa and Bidai tribes also lived in the territory, extending to the Old San Antonio Road. But they migrated, killed by other tribes or contracted diseases brought in by the Europeans. By the mid-1800s, they had disappeared.

The Spanish and Mexican authorities included colonization contracts for the future of Montgomery County. Forty-two families of Austin's colony settled there, one being Andrew Montgomery. And the county was born. Thick pine forests covered most of the county, with lumbering becoming its chief primary industry after 1900. Oil and gas discovery brought thousands to the area.

The Woodlands is considered fairly "new" as a city. It is twenty-five miles north of downtown Houston along I-45 and began as one of the nation's first-planned communities. George P. Mitchell founded The Woodlands in 1972, and it progressed from there.

An RX for Murder

A pharmacist is frequently the drugstore manager and closes the store at night as soon as customers leave the store. On the night of September 21, 1996, the night manager of Walgreens Drugstore on Sawdust Road in The Woodlands, had the responsibility of locking up. I will refer to him as Doug—even though his real name is a matter of public record.

As his family and friends verified, he was a friendly, easy-going young man who didn't have enemies. Former employees have said he had a sense of humor, which sometimes led to his playing tricks, like dropping a package of Huggies® on the floor, or calling someone to the phone when no one was on the line.

Doug had worked at another Walgreens for about ten years. He actually asked for a transfer to the Sawdust Road store, because he felt it would be safer than the former location. Unfortunately, this was not the case. Pharmacies and large drugstores keep quantities of prescription drugs on the premises, so they are a top priority for robbery.

Employees other than the pharmacist or manager sometimes open the stores. So the following morning, the employee who opened the store discovered Doug's lifeless body. He had been beaten, then shot.

If Doug had already locked the door before completing the day's receipts, how did someone get in? It would be unthinkable for Doug to leave the store without seeing the counters free of clutter—everything neat for the next day. He didn't have a chance to do that before he died. The perplexing question is why was there no forced entry?

Activity at Walgreens became a little unnerving. Schepp's Dairy offered a $10,000 reward, which they hoped would lead to the arrest and indictment of the murderer or murderers. Someone apparently took the bait about seven months later. An arrest followed. Two young men, charged with capital murder, went to trial.

Now, about why everything was void of a struggle when Doug was killed. The two young men, nineteen and twenty years of age, had been best friends through high school. And, the younger one, Eddie, actually worked part-time at the drugstore. He even worked the same day of the murder.

Doug would not have had reason to suspect him of anything, let alone a murder. Eddie had managed to get his friend, Jim, into the store before closing time. The idea was for Jim to hold them both up, making Eddie appear innocent. But something went wrong with their plan. Jim became nervous and shot Doug in the head.

They both ran with the $3,000 they'd stolen. Since there was no forced entry, the police became suspicious of Eddie. After their capture, the two went on trial for murder. Eddie maintained no one was to have been hurt. He just wanted the money. He claimed Jim pulled the trigger.

The police first tried Jim on a murder charge. In February 1998, the jury gave him life in prison. Putting the pieces together, the police charged Eddie with robbery only, since he testified against Jim as the triggerman. He received a twenty-five-year sentence.

Strange things took place at Walgreens soon after the trial. Employees reported that prescription bottles flipped off the shelves and battery-operated toys moved when no one turned them on. Yes, that could be unnerving. Items fell onto the floor, including disarrayed packages of diapers when the store opened in the mornings. The diaper thing was an occurrence when the haunting stories began, and employees thought at first that someone was playing a joke.

Through the years, weird incidents have almost ceased. When I spoke with the current pharmacist, he said nothing eerie has happened since he's been there. Prescription bottles remain on the shelves unless someone drops one by accident. Still, employees who were not there in 1996 noted an ethereal presence during their workday—cold spots, although the store had an evenly controlled thermostat.

Walgreens architectural remodeling hasn't reached this one-story building at the north end of a shopping strip. If Doug's spirit is an occasional visitor, he wouldn't mind. He would feel right at home. Incidentally, all the Huggies looked neatly arranged on the shelves when I was there.

> Walgreens
> 485 Sawdust Road
> The Woodlands, Texas 77380

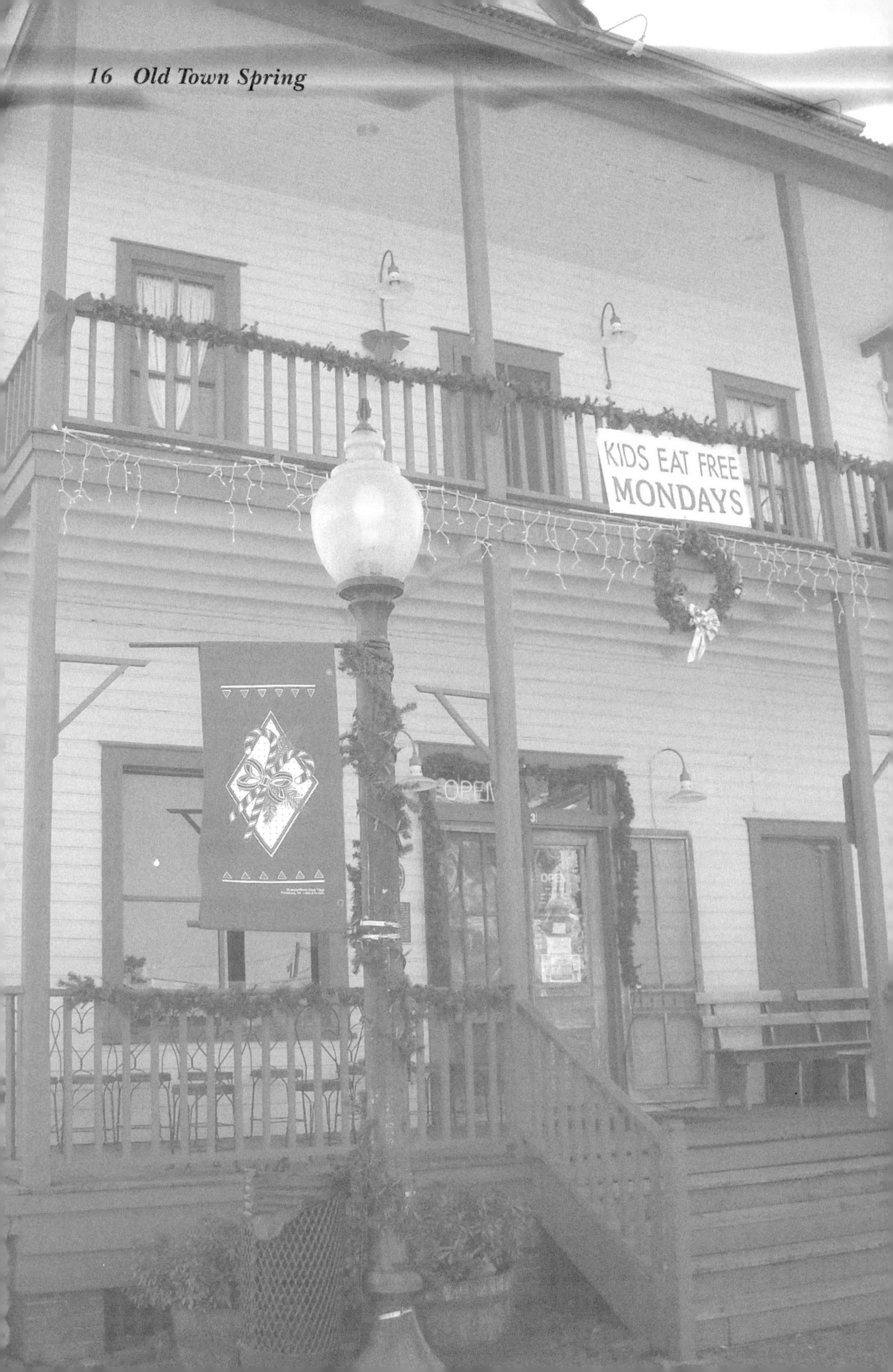
KIDS EAT FREE
MONDAYS
OPEN

OLD TOWN SPRING

Step back into time to one of the most unique turn-of-the-century (that other century) Texas communities. Old Town Spring is a fanciful escape into small towns of Texas past, just twenty minutes north of Houston. It's an old railroad village, reminding me of a Texas *Brigadoon*, the Scottish hamlet that came alive every hundred years.

When Texas won its Independence from Mexico in 1836, colonization flourished. After the Civil War, railroads expanded into South Texas and many more settlers arrived. The story goes that railroad workers named the town while laying tracks to the south during a brutal winter. By the time they finished in the springtime, their excitement caused them to name their destination "Camp Spring." It became a settlement in 1873, at which time they dropped "Camp" from the name. Being a base of operation, lumber companies, and farming, the town brought about opportunities for new immigrants.

Fast forward to 1902 when Spring prospered with an opera house, an assortment of businesses, and the Wunsche Bros. Café and Saloon. Success faltered when the railroad relocated to Houston. Many businesses closed, but the café and saloon held out the longest before shutting down. But now, they're all back—just like windmills.

After the Great Depression, as certain as spring follows winter, the bad times faded. You can now read about the history and see its reality for yourself. Take in the antique stores, art galleries, and craft shops, but be sure to visit the Historical Museum.

Turn east off I-45 onto Old Cypress Road. This nostalgic town has its own ghosts and is modern with a historical atmosphere. It appears to be a hamlet of the past, with tree-lined streets and friendly people. While the latter may go home at night and sleep, there's no telling what the residents of a ghostly form are up to.

The businesses are in separate small buildings, or, in most cases, small houses. You can bear toward the right and drive around before stopping. Be careful while trying to take in all you see on both sides. If you're early, you can find a convenient parking space. Additional parking is by the tracks, and signs lead to other areas. Don't forget to notice a cul de sac or two, tucked between and behind other businesses.

OLD AND OLDER

As you drive into Old Town Spring, the quaint white museum full of pictures and memorabilia will greet you. This nostalgic place has its own ghosts of days gone by.

After the museum staff locks the doors for the night, music wafts from a window in Old Town Spring's Museum. But no one is there to turn on the hand-cranked Victrola. The museum is haunted, you know.

Marie Bailey, who lived in St. Louis, had a sweetheart named Albert Paetzold. Her father did not approve of him. She was afraid of what her father might do to Albert, were he to spend more time with her. Marie had

Do phonograph needles last forever?

a mind of her own and continued with plans to marry. A young woman in love, she traveled from St. Louis to Spring to meet her sweetheart. Along with luggage, she managed to bring her Victrola.

There is often more than one version of a story. A particular one, according to Randy Woods, director of Old Town Spring's Walking Tour, makes perfect sense. The two young lovers, Marie and Albert, continued to live in exile. They lived in a farmhouse and spent many evenings dancing to music. The couple must have used a large amount of phonograph needles through the years, and there appears to be an unending supply.

When the couple "left" this earth, the Victrola became the property of the Lemm family. Later it belonged to the Mallotts, who donated it to the Historical Museum, where it is a favorite attraction.

Members of the Old Town Spring Historical Society operate the museum. When they turn off the lights and leave the building, they hear melodious strains coming from the hand-cranked Victrola. Others have said the record player switched itself on, even though the tunes sounded a little scratchy.

Not only do they hear music, but some people have reported viewing a couple waltzing inside. They see them through the window. The young woman wears her white satin bridal dress, a design of earlier times. Albert and Marie are dancing in the dark . . . wondering why they're there . . . time rushes by . . . are they really there?

Spring Historical Museum
403 Main Street
Old Town Spring, Texas 77373
281-651-0055
www.explorespring.com

SARAH! . . . WHERE A-R-E YOU?

Once upon a time, there was a little girl named Sarah, who lived in Spring. She was an active child. I can visualize her with blonde pigtails and blue ribbons—maybe freckles tossed across her nose. Sarah died over seventy-five years ago, but some say she is still here and have even seen her apparition.

Charles Wunsche in Old Town Spring sold land to Mary Kelly in 1881. Mary sold it to M. E. Hamilton. By 1917, he had built an impressive house on the land. He also built a large barn. At that time, barns were not unusual if the property lay on the outer edge of a town. Old Town Spring just sprang up around it.

Later on, Henry C. Doering and his wife, Ella Klein, bought the property from Mr. Hamilton and named it "Doering Court." Unfortunately, Henry succumbed to pneumonia in 1940, leaving his wife to take care of the home and their four offspring. From necessity, his widow rented the upstairs to railroad workers. She had no problem doing so, since the depot was close to their house. After Mr. Doering died, his widow lived in the home for thirty-three years, until her death.

When their children lived there, they found the barn and its loft a great place to play. They loved to run around a nearby haystack. You know, that huge mound of hay where the cows ate as high as they could until it looked like a giant mushroom. Or perhaps when *you* were a youngster, haystacks had already hidden their last needle, and rolled bales had taken over. But the tragedy in this story happened in the barn.

Friends came over and joined the children in their fun. They especially liked playing hide-and-seek. The youngest, Marilyn, had a best friend named Sarah. No one recalls her last name. The kids would run and giggle, then climb the ladder into the loft, where hay was stored.

One day when they were chasing each other, Sarah took a tumble and fell to the ground.

Marilyn ran for her friend's mother while the other children tried to make Sarah comfortable.

Her leg was badly broken, perhaps even in more than one place.

The doctor set the leg, but for some reason he couldn't diagnose, it became infected. The medical world has progressed in the last decades, but not in time for Sarah. She died of blood poisoning a few months later, at the age of twelve.

The story is, Sarah had not finished playing in real life. Maybe it was her turn to hide, and she still waits for the other girls to come over and play tag.

The owner of "Connie's Bath Shack," next door to the Doering House on Midway, pointed out the barn to me where Sarah fell, located on the west side of the backyard. It's painted red with white trim. Can't miss it from the street. Flower-filled window boxes and benches welcome you into the house, occupied by "The Dug Out," a shop of sports memorabilia & gifts. This was fitting—Sarah always was athletic.

Doering Court incorporates about six businesses in separate buildings. Through the years, people who have worked in the main house say they've heard sounds of giggling children. And even Sarah's

Sarah still plays in the barn.

name. "Sarah . . . Where a-r-e you?" The game of hide-and-seek has never ended. She was quiet the day I was there.

When Randall Woods first moved his newspaper office into the original barn, the previous business owner said, "By the way, this place is haunted." An interesting comment, which Mr. Woods didn't take too seriously at the time.

Soon after he moved in, Mrs. Woods brought her husband a ficus tree for the office. Sun shown through the window one afternoon. A wind picked up and the room grew cold. Even with the windows closed, a curious thing occurred. The leaves on the ficus tree fluttered. No other movement in the room—just the leaves.

Woods smiled and said, half-jokingly, "Sarah, if that's you, cut it out."

The leaves suddenly stopped moving, and the room temperature rose to normal. Although Randall Woods had always had an interest in the paranormal, it was that afternoon he began thinking there was something to this "ghost" lore, and he began to research. He formed the Old Town Spring Walking Tours of haunted places.

He told me that while at his desk, he occasionally felt a cold rush of air around him, even on a warm day. When someone left a pen in its holder or paper clips in the desk drawer, he would find the pen moved to another table and the clips scattered on his desk the following morning. He was a little suspicious that the mischievous Sarah was at play.

Woods has published *The Old Town Spring Newspaper* for several years, keeping everyone up to date on the "goings-on" of this special community.

So far, Sarah hasn't appeared in person to the publisher, but if one day in his new office, he feels a tap on his shoulder? "Tag, you're IT!"

Doering Court
The Dug Out
211-R Midway
Old Town Spring, Texas 77373

Spring State Bank

The Spring State Bank started off with a bang. It began with a capital of $10,000, a more than respectable sum for 1910. Actually, the real bangs didn't happen until 1932 after the town had blossomed with boarding houses, saloons—businesses that form an active community. With all the farming products and commercial interests because of the railroad, the bank was a strong point of Old Town Spring.

One day in 1932, a threesome attempted to rob the bank. All the teller had to do was pull out the money and hand it over. But not this teller. Instead, he pulled out a revolver.

Threatened, the trio ran toward the door, the teller chasing them. Shooting developed, with bullet holes left as trophies in the outside wall. No one was injured, and the town claimed the teller a hero.

Three bullet holes are in the brick wall to the right of the front door as you look toward it, with the first about doorknob level. The other, near the light fixture, and the third a little higher.

The robbers needed target practice.

On another occasion, a couple bearing resemblance to Clyde Barrow and Bonnie Parker walked right in and robbed the bank. They left with $7,380. The legend is, a witness remembered helping a twosome, answering Bonnie and Clyde's description, get their Ford out of the mud near Spring Creek. The witness felt secure in his identification, since rumor had it that Clyde always preferred to steal a Ford.

While the bank was victim of several robberies in the 30s, the *Handbook of Texas* points out that Bonnie and Clyde actually missed this one.

The bullet holes are there.

The bank closed in December 1933. The building stood vacant off and on for the last few years, but for the most part, businesses have occupied it. The main uninvited guests have appeared in the form of apparitions—no cold spots, just outlines shaded in gray. An owner on one occasion said the form headed for what use to be the bank vault and disappeared before he got there.

Since the building is no longer a bank, you can "deposit" your money at Creations De Main, a gift shop offering bath products, home décor, and specialty beeswax candles. A sales rep showed me the two-ton bank vault built into a short wall of brick. Its opening looks something like a submarine hatch. It isn't a walk-in. You reach in, but it no longer serves as a safe.

Any vapor in this little "bank shop" might not come only from the shop's beeswax candles. With threatening activity in the bank's past, it seems natural the old building would be a deposit vault of residual energy, if not a little gunpowder residue from previous gunfire.

No one has reported any recent disturbances. Creations De Main has moved, having gone into the wholesale business, but that doesn't mean the ghosts have left the old bank. Since it's rumored a ghost might be loitering on the sidewalk near the entrance, even in the daytime, be cautious as you pass by.

(You can keep up with Creations De Main: www.CDMcandles. com.)

The Old Bank Building
115 Midway
Old Town Spring, Texas 77373

WHERE'S CHARLIE?

Customers at Wunsche Bros. Café & Saloon are aware of cold spots as they move from the bar to a table. Doesn't happen all the time—just occasionally. But it's no secret there is a presence there. The café is on the right at the end of Midway—a cream-colored wooden building with green trim.

Someone inhabited the area long before Stephen F. Austin's colonists arrived. The Orcoquiza Indians found it first. Eventually, German immigrants moved in and developed farmland.

The most prominent was farmer Carl Wunsche. He and his family emigrated from Germany to Texas in 1846. They operated a gristmill, gin, and later, a sawmill. His sons, Dell and Charlie, felt they could succeed in something other than farming, so chose to go into the saloon and hotel business. Actually, their young brother, William ("Willie"), was in on the first in-town business venture.

Entrepreneurs of the period, the Wunsches constructed their building on land their parents left them. They built it near the railroad to serve passengers as well as railroad employees.

According to tour guide, Randy Woods, Charlie thought he had found the love of his life, but she favored another and ran away with him. Poor Charlie was so distraught, he apparently didn't seek the love of anyone else and remained a bachelor the rest of his life.

People never knew if he was despondent, because he always seemed happy and cordial to the customers. He stopped by tables to see if anyone needed anything and was adamant about keeping the hotel rooms clean for the next guests. When not working, Charlie, affectionately called "Uncle Charlie," spent time in his upstairs hotel room where he lived. He loved this place. It was like a dream come true. He never really wanted to be a farmer in the first place.

But Charlie took sick and died in 1915. New owners took over the business and kept the name. From many accounts, Charlie was not ready to leave. Maybe he predicted the ensuing developments in Old Town Spring and wanted to keep an eye on his saloon.

Circumstances were bleak, especially after the rail yard moved to Houston in 1923. It didn't take long for the once-prosperous town of Spring to come to a near halt, as happened with a multitude of other small Texas communities. Wunsche Bros. was the last saloon to close during Prohibition. The Depression made matters worse, but once recovery began, the Saloon and Hotel surpassed previous success—the only saloon that had "held on tight."

As Randy Woods tells the legend, at that time, a struggling artist checked in at the hotel and spent the night in the same room in which Charlie had lived. He dreamed an old man sat in a chair, hunched over the table. The vision was so real he could even draw a picture of him. He brought out paper and pencil and worked from memory, sketching every detail.

The following day he showed the picture to the employees and other diners. Without hesitation, more than one exclaimed the guest had sketched Uncle Charlie with white hair, the black hat he often wore, and a black suit. They concluded Charlie might have resented someone sleeping in his bed. At any rate, the artist could not have known what Wunsche looked like.

That is the kind of story people can pass down year after year—and they do.

In 1949, Viola Burke operated the Saloon and Hotel under the name of The Spring Café, noted for its hamburgers that possibly resurrected the town of Spring. They were that good. Railroad workers hurried to put in their order before grabbing the next train out.

Scott and Brenda Mitchell purchased and refurbished the business in 1982, under its original name. Soon its reputation of atmosphere and fine food spread. At well over a hundred years old, it remains one of oldest buildings in town.

At that time, Willie, ninety-four-year-old grandson of Carl and Jane, and the son of William, told the Mitchells he was thirteen years old when his brothers built the saloon. He helped by carrying nails and lunch pails. He said Dell and Charlie used "heart lumber" (free of sapwood) cut at their own sawmill. They had their heart in their work, as well.

It's as if Wunsche Bros. marks the foundation around which other shops want to locate—over 150 of them. The café opens at 11:00, and by the time you've walked around this little town, you'll be ready for a Wunsche lunch.

Country music artists have played at the saloon, including Clint Black and Lyle Lovett.

National and state historic site markers stand outside the building. They still serve the best hamburgers around. Ice cream chairs are on the front porch, as well as on the upstairs wide balcony, where you can relax with a cold beer.

You can photograph this atmospheric piece of history in your mind, if you can look up long enough from their delectable Whiskey Chocolate Cake, "a dessert as dense and dark as midnight." That's how *Texas Monthly* describes it. Devilishly paranormal.

I have heard and read different versions of the story of the Wunsche Bros. Café and Saloon, and you possibly have, too. The previous owner had encountered Uncle Charlie several times. She would move furniture or other items, and he was apparently not happy with the change. Various objects disappeared or moved around, and she would find them in the most unexpected areas. That's why she tried to keep everything in its place, but when a new employee moved a table or chair, it would soon be back where it was.

On a still night, people say you can hear Uncle Charlie strolling from room to room—even up and down the stairs. He likes his rocking chair as much as he ever did. No one can see him. The chair simply rocks. But the facts seem always to be the same. This historic landmark is haunted. I'll stick with that.

Brother Charlie strolls through the café whenever he wants.

Wunsche Bros. Café & Saloon
103 Midway
Old Town Spring, Texas 77373
281-350-1902

Age Springs Eternal

Whooo . . . Whooo . . . "Down by the station, early in the morning..."
You know how the song goes: "See the little pufferbellies, all in a row."
These lyrics refer to a small pot-bellied steam engine, not "Thomas."

Fire destroyed the town's train station in the 1950s. In 1985, interested
buyers purchased the old station in the town of Lovelady. They separated
it into two sections, then moved it to 100 Main Street in Spring. It took

three nights to accomplish the feat. "Puffabelly" is the name given to the hundred-year-old structure.

The depot, representative of the prevalent small-frame designs of the period, offered the usual waiting and baggage areas (and a brass spittoon or two). Old pointed rooflines were almost always yellow and green, often with a red trim. The overhangs protected passengers as well as baggage. For almost ten years, when no longer used as a depot, it served as a storage area and a retail shop selling leather goods.

Restored in 1995, the building is now "Puffabellys Depot Café." Word is the food is great, and special live entertainment is booked on a regular basis. Local residents have reported seeing apparitions within its walls. Paranormal tales concerning Puffabellys originated in Lovelady and followed the little depot right on down the road as it moved to its new locale.

Legend has it that soon after the original structure's completion, a railroad switchman fell on the tracks as he ran, waving a lantern to warn of the oncoming train. The train failed to stop in time and ran over the switchman. The fact the accident decapitated him, produced

Down by the station. . . .

the tale that a headless man moves up and down the tracks, searching for . . . well, you know.

Once the depot moved to Spring, eerie sightings in Lovelady diminished. According to Randy Woods, weird incidents began to occur soon after Puffabellys Café opened. One gentleman reported seeing strange lights coming toward, or away, from the building. He felt certain a train would head down the tracks, but not so. There was no train—only the lights approaching, then disappearing. His was not the only report.

The sighting of lights near railroad tracks, especially when close to a cemetery, is not uncommon.

Old Town Spring likes the name, "The Ghost Capital of Texas," even though other towns also claim the title. Ghosts, however, seem to spring up all over Spring. There are people who have viewed the apparition of a soldier just after the area's Civil War Reenactment.

Puffabellys Depot Café is at the east end of Main Street, on a line with Wunsche Bros.

Stop by sometime and pay close attention to what you think you see—or know. Concentrate on the eastside of the building, near the tracks. You might just see the light.

Puffabellys Depot Cafe
100 Main Street
Old Town Spring, Texas 77373
281-350-3376
www.puffabellys.com

A House By Any Other Name

When in Old Town Spring, don't consider leaving until you've joined the Randall Woods' Tours. The bad news is, Whitehall is no longer open to tours at this time; but the good news is, Randy will escort you by the house and tell you more about its history.

Some of Austin's colonists settled in the area in the 1820s before it became a trading post in 1838. The town prospered after the Houston and Great Northern Railroad formed in 1873. A lumber mill thrived; stores and hotels popped up near the railroad tracks. If men didn't need a hotel room, they could make use of the many saloons. With a roundhouse and several track yards, railroad workers made up a sizeable population of their own.

The town had its day of saloon brawling to riotous behavior in general, both inside or on dusty streets. Many of the fine homes still exist, renovated and now lived in. Quaint cottages are homes to boutiques, gift shops, antiques, and the like. The proprietors unite in preserving the charm of their town.

If you were to ask, most shop owners would know of the ghosts, even if their own businesses never had visitors of the vaporous kind.

One of the more fascinating tales surrounds Whitehall, the two-story Victorian structure at Main and Keith Streets. On the corner, the house sits behind a white iron picket fence. It is now occupied by The Princess Bridal, offering bridal gowns, grooms' tuxedos, as well as full wedding plans.

It's had many occupants during its over 110-year lifespan, first as a residence for the Mintz family. With such a dense wooded area, lumber was readily accessible for a large house, and the cost was reportedly $300.

When the Mintzes left Whitehall, McGowen's Boarding House took over, a great convenience for the railroad workers. According to the history given by Mr. Woods, the Kleins, owners of the local funeral home, purchased it from the McGowens in the 1930s. The funeral home burned, so the family turned the downstairs rooms of Whitehall into the funeral parlor and embalming room.

At the arrival of prohibition, all businesses suffered. The Depression left only a few shops and one little depot, which eventually met its end by fire.

In the next ten years, because of World War II, the home converted into apartments. Later on, a church, then a school, followed by hippies—Spring's only commune. The Hudson family purchased it in the 1970s. They restored, redecorated, and offered it as a beautiful Victorian tour highlight.

Bluebonnets grow in the backyard, geraniums flourish in pots, and most unusual is the large dovecote incorporating the back corner two floors of the house. Different species of doves have lived there, with hanging baskets for their individual nesting condos.

Remains of a 1940s tree house still stand in the backyard, next to a pristine white gazebo.

A sign on the tree trunk lists original members of a kids' club. They were two brothers, a neighbor friend, a couple dogs, and an occasional visiting cat or two. This is what kids did before television and iPods®. An epilog on the sign was one brother later died in Korea, another became a lawyer, the friend left for East Texas, and the dogs are fond memories. The cats moved on.

Also on the sign is a note written by the owners:

"This house was never grand—just a simple and well-constructed building with one secret room, but tells no secrets. I see my home as a kind forgiving old lady—gone through many changes, tough times, stood tall and very proud."

~Harold and Deloris Hudson

A young man was taking his sweetheart for a drive late one evening in 1933. Somehow, he was distracted and ran the car off Spring Creek Bridge. Both young people died in the crash. Two passersby found them the next morning and transported the couple to the funeral home.

The belief is their spirits still linger in Whitehall. People have seen their apparitions swaying in a screened-in porch swing on the second floor.

Legend has it the young twosome "live" in the secret room referred to in the sign, coming out on moonlit nights. Some say they have seen them strolling in the garden. They possibly sit in the gazebo, holding hands and listening to the cooing of the doves.

And another thing—about a colony of bats in Whitehall's attic. Bats have long been associated with the spirit world. As long as these little guys circle in their own space, they don't bother anyone. We all know they're nocturnal, and you shouldn't reach out and touch one even if you could.

In Java, bats are a warning of death. Some cultures believe a bat is a symbol of longevity and happiness. People in Tonga and West Africa consider them a person's soul. But in Old Town Spring, can it be they are to remind us of the spirits that live there? Otherwise, they just sort of hang around. No bad raps for the bats.

Whitehall (The Princess Bridal)
Main and Keith Street
Old Town Spring, Texas 77373
281-651-9393
www.theprincesbridal.com

CROSBY

Crosby is two miles north of State Highway 90, outside Houston city limits, in the Newport Subdivision. Humphrey Jackson, one of the original 300 colonists settling Texas, founded the settlement in 1823. Prior to the Civil War, the site that became Crosby was nicknamed "Lick Skillet," coming from team drivers sipping sweet spring water and "licking their skillets clean."

Settlers named the town for G. J. Crosby, a railroad construction engineer. As soon as the railroad arrived, it became a shipping center for agricultural and lumber products.

After the Civil War, plantation owners allowed free black slaves burial rights on property they had previously worked on. Years later when the property was sold, it appeared no one mentioned the burial ground. But according to *Wikipedia*, upon development of the area, a contractor searched for a gravedigger who told them the houses would be on top of the cemetery.

ANTS AND SNAKES AND GHOSTS, OH MY!

A book about the haunted coastal areas of Texas would not be complete without the story of poltergeists, flying black insects, and frenzied pets. To top it all off, the house in question stood over an old slave graveyard called "The Black Hope Cemetery." But who knew? The Purcell Corporation bought the land in the Newport Subdivision for residential development. Could it be they thought the few worn crosses in the area meant nothing? Or, as long as they weren't digging too far beneath the soil, it didn't matter if they built houses on a graveyard. Each time a train ran the tracks over a graveyard, it rattled the bones of our ancestors.

Still happens.

Horrifying incidents occurred with one of the first houses sold on the street in the Newport Subdivision—to Ben and Jean Williams. The homes at the same end of the street, however, also created such uneasiness and fear, the owners quickly put their homes up for sale. People moved in. People moved out just as fast.

The Williamses had filled their moving van and moved into their dream house in 1983.

From the beginning, they noticed the weird carvings on an oak tree in their yard but soon disregarded them. Besides, the beautiful tree cast shade over the living-room window. Jane chose to keep the tree, although others on the lots were cut down.

 Not easy, or even possible to understand, were the moving shadows throughout the house, unknown voices; footsteps after everyone had retired for the night. Some might dismiss the latter as merely echoing sounds from the street, but not Ben and Jean Williams. After they leveled the lot for landscaping and planted grass, sinkholes appeared. As in a cemetery, after topsoil has settled, a low place develops above the gravesite. New grass usually levels it, but not in this case.

The builders treated houses for termites, sprayed for insects; still, insects swarmed through the home, even though doors were shut and windows sealed. The washing machine stopped and started. Ants traveled in and out of the dishwasher.

For Ben and Jane, pets had died. Snakes slithered down the hallway. A kind of thick liquid reportedly oozed from the wall. Their garage doors opened by themselves. Electrical appliances turned on, whether the family wanted toast or not.

The fact their house and perhaps small parts of others were constructed over a cemetery, presented its full impact when neighbors decided to have a swimming pool. The realization that disturbing long-dead bodies buried in the yard had caused the horrendous experiences, surfaced when two skeletons were uncovered in the excavating process for the pool.

My friends for several years, Pete and Carolyn Haviland, of *Lone Star Spirits*, headed an investigation. They and their team ventured into the then-wooded area across the street from Ben and Jane's house. At sunset, several black forms encircled them—the same kind that appeared in the home of the Williamses.

Haviland said he made eye-contact with one of the eerie forms, just before feeling a sharp numbness all over and a tightening in his stomach, topped off with a stunning pain in his neck. They chose this as a good time to leave. Pete and his team made additional investigations, observing little the second time. The third visit, it was as if the black figures had waited to greet them, and then disappeared.

Close friends and neighbors of the Williamses, had experienced similar situations. Ben and Jane had enough. Above all, their young daughter died a mysterious death. She was recovering from an undiagnosed illness when she died of a massive heart attack, believed to have been brought on by fear.

There was only one decision for Ben and Jane to make—leave the home they had saved for years to buy. Nothing could undo the trauma the Williamses experienced in their dream house, but they wanted to remind people such things do happen. They wrote a bestseller about their horrendous experiences: *The Black Hope Horror: The True Story of a Haunting.*

Apparently, paranormal events on this street in Crosby have settled down over the past few years. An occasional report from the neighborhood comes in to the police department. Upon investigation, the officers usually find a false alarm—no one in the house. Minor occurrences such as a television turning on and off, with no human responsible, might alarm a resident enough to call 911. That in itself isn't so much, but under the circumstances. . . .

If their story doesn't prime your paranormal imagination, nothing will. Listen! . . . What was that eerie humming sound coming from the hallway?

> Newport Subdivision
> The street known as "Poppet's Way"
> Crosby, Texas 77532

LIBERTY

Liberty is the seat of Liberty County on State Highway 146 and U.S. Highway 90.

American squatters occupied the land in 1818 when Spanish law still controlled it. The community, first known as *Villa de la Santisima Trinidad de la Libertad*, changed to Liberty after so many settlers migrated from Liberty, Mississippi.

Sam Houston practiced law in the community from the 1830s to the 1850s and owned two plantations until his death.

According to *The Handbook of Texas*, captured Mexican officers of the Battle of San Jacinto remained prisoners for a while in William Hardin's homestead, later known as Mexican Hill. Harriet Paine, a slave of Hardin's, treated the prisoners kindly. She lived to be almost 100 years old and offered much to the area's folklore and history. All those with whom she came in contact, loved her.

The Liberty Invincibles organized in 1861, with many area citizens enlisting. The railroad suspended operations but had resumed by 1875. Schools shut down for a time during reconstruction. In 1866 and 1867 yellow fever and smallpox epidemics slowed progress, especially the area's leading cotton crop.

During World War II, the Liberty fairgrounds served as a camp for German prisoners of war. The nearby home of Governor M. Price Daniel, Sr., built in 1984, is based on the original plans for the Governor's Mansion in Austin.

THE HISTORIC OTT HOTEL

The new owners had no clue, when they purchased property from the Ott family in 2002, what they were getting into. They knew the large hotel, which opened in 1928, was just what they were looking for.

Thing is, they were not looking for ghosts. When they purchased the hotel, they gave it a thorough cleaning and general fixing up. They also became acquainted with more permanent guests, those who had "lived" there for decades. Now that they've been there a while, they are perfectly willing to discuss tales of not only their own ghostly experiences but those of guests as well. With such history surrounding Liberty, Texas, no one would be surprised if ghosts inhabit the community, with the Ott Hotel the center of interest.

The Ott has many tales to tell.

Oil was the up and coming attraction in the late 1920s when the county experienced the development of a large number of oil fields. It couldn't have come at a better time. And with the new economy turned on by agriculture and trade, the town needed a hotel in the worst way.

John Joshua Ott of Louisiana and his wife, Sallie Wiggins, of San Jacinto, chose a site for a hotel and contracted Elza Burch to build it. As in most towns in those days, a hotel stood near the train depot. Mr.

Ott geared his toward traveling salesmen, called "drummers." They could debark the train and take a room close by. They often had appointments with prospective customers right in the "drummer's room," set aside for their displays of wares.

With a wide front porch, hotel guests could watch traffic pass by, as well as see their trains come in—to know if they were on schedule. Trains ran the tracks thirty or forty times a day, and are still in use, although not so much now.

The original design included fifty rooms with community baths in the middle of long halls. The hotel proved so necessary and popular, some of the parlor and dining-room space was transformed into additional guest rooms.

The first indication that ghosts inhabited the Ott came from an occurrence in 1930.

Jealousy was the root of the tragic tale. In late fall, a couple had engaged a room. The two were married—but not to each other. Anna obviously thought her husband, Joshua, had no idea about the rendezvous she had with her lover at the hotel. Perhaps she didn't give him enough credit.

Joshua found out about the affair and stormed off to confront them. Having no idea in which room they were, he knocked on each door, startling the guests. Eventually, he rattled the right one. Sylvia opened it. Once Joshua saw his wife standing there in a white nightgown, my guess is he knew right then his wife wasn't at the hotel for a business meeting.

Everyone in the hotel could hear the two arguing. A momentary silence. Then . . . a shot.

Anna and her lover lay dead in the hallway. The fact the same bullet killed both of them was remarkable. People poured from their rooms to see Anna's husband rush down the stairs.

They noted the man wore a black cowboy hat, black boots, and a duster.

In November when the blustery wind blows, faint echoes of an argument drift through the second-floor hall. If you're very quiet at just the right time, you can hear a single shot. By chance, if you don't hear it, you might sense the faint smell of gunpowder.

Several rooms have ghostly visitors, with 101, 103, 107, 206, 214, and 216 high in activity. One group of paranormal investigators stayed in the latter two rooms. Their electro-magnetic readings were off the wall. Paranormal groups have found amazing results with their cameras and recorders—anomalies and unknown voices.

A gentleman guest had brought his new cell phone/camera along and was reading directions. He accidentally clicked the shutter. Upon replay, the picture showed a well-dressed woman standing by the dresser. Wanting to tell someone what he had seen, he hurried downstairs to show the management and other guests. They were equally impressed.

The manager asked to download the picture to the office computer. A guest tried to download it to his cell phone. Neither worked. During the night, a couple days later, the guest, his wife, and their daughter, left. Something strange must have happened, but he never said.

A security videotape installed in the upstairs hallway shows the staircase door shut. No one walked through the hall, but the tape is proof the door will open and close during the night. The audiotape at the same place had recorded voices, mostly argumentative, but no one is there. Again, proved by the video.

On one occasion, a guest walked down the stairs when he felt someone pulling his coat. At least that's what it seemed to him. He thought his coat might have caught on something, but he found no nail or hook of any kind. He continued down the remaining steps and felt the same sensation. There was never an explanation.

One owner told me of other poltergeist activity. An item flew off the mantle to the floor. A piece of glassware shattered on the floor when no one was near. She feels someone is just endeavoring to attract attention. Since the ghosts are benevolent, she thinks there is apparently nothing to fear.

There have been nine deaths in the hotel through the years, having nothing to do with ghosts . . . I think. The scent of roses and patchouli is not unnoticed, and a spirit also leaves behind the smell of cigar smoke. They named him "Bob." Or, rather, an apartment tenant of twelve years, named the ghost that long ago.

Opposite page:
Guests hear rushed footsteps on the stairs.

Another cell-phone picture was sure to prove a ghost was present. A couple who left the coastline during Hurricane Rita, checked in at the Ott. While they used their cell to call family, an apparition appeared in front of them. The guest snapped a picture and hurried downstairs to tell the McCains. He had clearly seen the apparition on the photo, but when he came downstairs, the phone was dead. No picture. No working battery, even though he had just charged it.

Portions of the Ott have recently been renovated. They have seven bedrooms and ten large one-bedroom efficiency apartments. While they were refurbishing a downstairs apartment, two guests stopped in disbelief. One of them questioned the other, wondering if he had seen the same thing he had. Turns out, they each had witnessed a half-body apparition of a nice-looking man wearing a blue shirt. The McCains call him the "Blue Man."

Residents, the staff, other help and maintenance workers, have all reported weird experiences: Doors opening and closing, knocking when no one is there. And there's Stinky Bob, a ghost with a scent of decay.

As I was typing the last of this story, Susan McCain phoned me. She had just come from room 206, calming a guest who was distressed because a spectral man was in her room. Susan moved the woman down the hall.

She then reminded "Joshua," the name given to this wandering ghost, wearing a black hat, duster coat and boots, that he shouldn't bother the guests. Won't do too much good. He was the one who murdered his wife and continues to drop in on lady guests. Joshua could possibly be looking for his wife? To apologize, or shoot her again?

The hotel kitty, named "Miracle," is a survivor of Ike. No bad luck with this little black cat.

The storm of September 2008 blew off the roof of a large storage barn housing furniture and other items. During the aftermath of the storm, many displaced persons found rooms at the Ott. The McCains have repaired all damage now, so consider the Historic Ott Hotel an important stopover on your next vacation. It has recently received a Historical Marker of the State of Texas. Think how important those spirits feel now.

The Historic Ott Hotel
305 Travis
Liberty, Texas 77575
936-336-3832
www.hauntedotthotel.com

SEVEN PINES

This is a story centering on Christy, the son of Benjamin Hardin and his wife, Cynthia O'Brien, and also on Harriett, the family's devoted slave. And it is Christy who won't leave.

Benjamin Franklin (Frank) Hardin and his wife, and his four brothers, settled in the Mexican state of Coahuila, later becoming Liberty County. They all developed plantations along the Trinity River. Before 1830 the brothers' parents journeyed to Texas to join them. Several slaves, including Harriet, accompanied the Hardins.

About 1839, Frank and his vivacious wife, Cynthia, planned and built their dream house, "Seven Pines," in which members of the family lived for four generations. Frank was a participant in the Battle of San Jacinto and a commander of the Home Guard in the 1840s.

Harriet tended the needs of the Hardins. She and her two children lived in a house at the back of Seven Pines. Harriett, known as "Miss Thimble," made shirts for the "men" in the family, as well as sewing for the girls.

Because of the brothers' accomplishments, Hardin County bears their name. Each of them earned his respected reputation in the community long after the Civil War, further cementing their connection to home and family. The townspeople had nothing but praise, especially for Frank Hardin and his fair treatment of his slaves.

Frank and Cynthia had six children: Sons, Bee and Christy, and daughters, Camilla, Mimmie, Nannie, and Shattee. They attended a one-teacher school near their home. All the siblings had equally likeable personalities.

While Bee and Christy set traps as boys, their sister Mimmie gathered eggs and was proud of the twenty-seven hens in her care. The brothers were never at a loss to find something to do as youngsters—after they did their chores. Fifty or sixty Indians camped in the area but never presented trouble. Going to town to watch Indians play a certain kind of Indian Ball was one form of entertainment the boys enjoyed.

Sister Shattee was particularly fond of her brother, Christy. When she was at school, he wrote letters to her about the horse he tried to break and what everybody was doing. He also mentioned their mother had her "regulator" cane hanging on the wall and, on occasion, "hauled" it down upon them. As Christy grew older, he tended the farm and saw to his father's pasture.

Uppermost on his mind was enlisting in the army. He had been gathering beef for the army since he was sixteen and wanted to be a soldier. The war became full blown, but until Christy came of age to enlist, he continued with his schooling.

Inflation was rampant during the war. All items were scarce, not even shoes to buy. Frank learned to make shoes for his family, and even though they resembled moccasins, they served the purpose. His peach and corn crops froze. Cynthia dyed thread to make shirts for Bee and Christy.

When Bee, two years older than Christy, came of age, he enlisted in the army. He received orders to go to Mud Island, near Galveston. When Christy turned 18, he joined.

After Lee surrendered at Appomattox on April 9, 1865, the official surrender in Texas occurred on June 2. Christy would soon join Bee, a sergeant and a paroled prisoner of war.

Many released prisoners returned to Mexico, although scores also settled in Texas. The kind treatment given them by the Hardins and Aunt Harriet influenced their decision to stay. Harriet seemed to have an unexplained magic, with the wisdom to help others, no matter who they were. She delighted them with stories, as well as her general manner.

Frank and Cynthia hosted a large party in appreciation for friends who showed support for their sons. The party was successful, but any zest for life after the war, had faded for Bee. His world had changed. He had chosen to study law but took to alcohol. He never found a young lady with whom to share his life. He chose, instead, to shut out the world and embrace the love and peace that Seven Pines offered him.

The other siblings went on with their lives, and eventually, Bee went back to his law practice. His father felt it was imperative to do so. "Open wounds needed to heal." Some of the soldiers could not adjust to the life they left before the war.

But Christy, a blue-eyed blond adored by his family came home from the war, happy to be there, and with no problems. Two winters after his discharge, he was out hunting. His companion, thinking a movement in the woods was a deer, fired. He fired one shot, then the realization came to him like a thunderbolt. Christy fell dead.

No one could believe it happened, and certainly not after the young man came safely home from the war.

After Christy's sister, Camilla, married George Davis, they moved into Seven Pines, where Aunt Harriet continued to care for the family. After Camilla's daughter, Geraldine, married George Humphreys, they lived in the Pines. Frank had died in 1878 and Cynthia, 1889.

Years later, in 1916, a chimney fire almost destroyed the house. Harriet came to the rescue in saving family letters and documents that she had saved in a safe cupboard. She knew so much, she could answer any questions about the family. Harriet remained in the house behind Seven Pines. She died the year after the fire, almost 100 years old.

As Aunt Harriet, a wise woman and one who had absorbed so much in her long life, consistently said, "I seen Christy's ghost again last night down by the gate. He can't rest."

Harriet mentioned it many times.

But what became of the letters? Camilla Davis Trammell, granddaughter of Geraldine Humphreys, acquired them, as a gift from a cousin. Mrs. Trammell compiled the correspondence into a memorable book, *Seven Pines: Its occupants and their letters, 1925-1872*.

The paranormal content is as strong as the reader wishes. It was meaningful to Aunt Harriet. The beautiful home no longer stands on the site. In its place is The Geraldine D. Humphreys Cultural Center.

If you visit the Center, or even walk quietly by, pay close attention to any vaporous mist. It may be blond, blue-eyed Christy Hardin, who died too young at the age of twenty. Aunt Harriet could be right. Christy is still there.

Geraldine D. Humphreys Cultural Center
1710 Sam Houston Street
Liberty, Texas 77575
936-336-8901

HOUSTON

When I first visited Houston to research this book, the city showed little proof that a harrowing storm had blown through only six weeks earlier. I was aware of sidewalk trees broken to the ground, and boards still covered windows in the upper floors of Houston's tallest building, the Chase Tower. Witnesses had viewed furniture and computers plummeting out the windows, along with glass crashing to the sidewalks. The rain fell straight down until the wind turned it horizontal, like trillions of darts.

That doesn't diminish the damage Ike had accomplished elsewhere in the city. Much of Houston was "out of commission" for many days—no water, no heat, no electricity. Tree surgeons and other citizens cut 5.6 million cubic yards of wood debris from broken trees and limbs. After recycling, the wood chips could "fill the Astrodome four times."

Mayor Bill White announced, "We will recall the hardships and the recovery . . . And most of all, let us share stories of how we helped each other through this mess."

A little history of Houston . . . In 1836, brothers Augustus C. and John K. Allen founded this fertile land near the banks of Buffalo Bayou. The brothers were real estate entrepreneurs who came to Texas from New York with the idea in mind to establish a city. And that they did.

They named it after General Sam Houston, the president of the Republic of Texas.

The city fathers realized how important it would be to promote a shipping business. And, by 1860, Houston was the shipping hub for exporting cotton. After the Civil War, businessmen furthered their efforts to develop more commerce between Houston and the port of Galveston. And there it began. . . .

In 1902, Teddy Roosevelt okayed a $1 million improvement for the Houston Ship Channel. During the twentieth century, Houston has become the home of the world's largest healthcare institution and NASA's Johnson Space Center. When built, Houston's Astrodome was known as the "Eighth Wonder of the World." The city has suffered and recovered from hurricanes, the Enron collapse, and growing pains, to become the largest city in the state and the fourth largest in the country.

And oh, yes, home to many revenants in various spirit forms.

If you are unfamiliar with downtown Houston, be prepared for the one-way streets. I feel reasonably sure I'd still be there were it not for the chattering lady on my GPS. As I was ready to find Rusk Street, she told me more than once she'd lost her satellite connections (those Texas skyscrapers). C'mon, lady, the light's turning green. I thought I detected panic in her voice. She pulled herself together and told me to turn right . . . Made it!

A Red Sequin, and More

Ghosts in the University of Houston tend to center around specific buildings on campus. Students studying late can verify unexplained goings-on in the Cullen building. They can't account for them. Custodians know ghosts are there. And who is the woman in the red dress?

It seems revenants wait until humans leave a place for the night before they begin to wander, or they might wander right before closing. Apparently they want someone to be aware of their presence, just not everyone.

The Hugh Roy and Lillie Cullen Building is one of the most recognizable in Central Texas. The structure is now included in the National Registry of Historic Sites. Born in 1881, Hugh Roy was the grandson of Ezekial W. Cullen, who migrated to Texas from Georgia in 1835, during the days pioneers moved westward to seek their fame and fortune. He fought in the revolution against Mexico, and afterward, settled in San Augustine to watch his dream come true.

Hugh Roy formed his own oil companies and became one of the richest men in America.

After losing their only son, Roy Gustav, in an oil field accident, Hugh and his wife contributed a total of $335,000 for the first permanent building on the University of Houston campus, in Roy Gustav's memory.

The Cullens loved the university and could see it as a place for young people to acquire sound educations. Spirits may have sought that same goal. Hugh Roy contributed $160 million to create the Cullen Foundation. One could say he was possessed of a giving spirit.

The Ezekiel W. Cullen building has been on campus for over sixty years. Built in 1948, it was set up with a proscenium stage. The dedication date? Halloween 1950. Who knows if this date brought about part of the folklore surrounding this building as well as other Cullen edifices on campus.

According to Manuel Rearte, who wrote for *The Daily Cougar*, unidentifiable noises come from the crawl space beneath the seating area of the auditorium. That kind of occurrence would tend to unnerve an audience, especially if the performance was *The Phantom of the Opera*.

Winding hallways, stairwells, and hidden passageways—particularly the latter—offer a simple route for any ghost to move about the theatre. But who, or what, lingers in this building? And why, is an intriguing question. Some people believe the ghost of Hugh Roy Cullen wanders through the basement levels of the auditorium. Others have reason to believe his spirit strolls throughout the Performance Hall, keeping watch over every aspect of its operation.

Members of the Residual Energy Investigators studied the ghosts of the Performance Hall.

Robert Hernandez, graduate of the University of Houston, and also a member of REI, interviewed Sidney Berger, former director of the School of Theatre. Mr. Berger said he taught a student in the 1970s, who was involved in a late-night rehearsal. She said she had seen ". . . what looked like a Spanish soldier in full uniform."

Mr. Berger told the student the building had been constructed over a burial ground for Spanish soldiers. That might activate a ghost or two—as in the haunting of Texas Wesleyan Fine Arts Building in Fort Worth, or The Black Hope Horror. Nothing like a ghost wanting a breath of fresh air.

Hernandez and his team members set up infrared cameras, laser temperature readers, electromagnetic field detectors—all the equipment necessary for at least a two-hour stay to detect what paranormal activity might show up.

As shown from the experiences of many paranormal investigators, or individuals who are checking out haunted places, spirits tend to drain energy from cameras, batteries, and other electrical equipment. This was the case with the Residual Energy Investigators when they visited the Cullen building. A team member said three cameras broke on them.

According to an article written by Steve Boss, staff reporter for the *University of Houston Communication Network*, ghosts wander up and down halls of this landmark. When anyone investigates unusual sounds in specific rooms, nothing is inside. Custodians trying to finish tasks early can't always avoid a ghost's presence. They hear slamming doors when no one is there to slam them, nor is there a suction caused by wind.

Legend tells us a workman fell to his death from the roof during the building's construction. If this is true, employees believe the man's spirit returns to finish his work. As Gram Gemoets, news reporter for *The Daily Cougar*, said, "Maintenance personnel claim to hear the eerie pound of a phantom hammer."

A custodian later vowed to have seen the ghost a few years earlier. He kept hearing a "clicking noise." He turned around and viewed an apparition floating past him. The custodian "ran and didn't look back."

The weirdest occurrence, aside from the spirit of Hugh Roy, is a female ghost said to make frequent "appearances" in the corridors and in the women's restroom of the Cullen Performance Hall. She always drops, either on purpose or accidentally, a red sequin on the floor as she leaves. The "suspects" for the lady in red? Some believe she is Mrs. Hugh Roy Cullen, possibly having worn a red dress for the opening of the Cullen Building.

If Mrs. Cullen, however, felt a red sequin dress not appropriate, there is another scenario.

A performer, once appearing on the proscenium stage, could have loved the theatre and never wanted to leave. Chances are we will never learn her identity. If pictures are in the archives, a former actress may have worn a red sequined dress.

During evening classes, students usually attend in pairs. If they hear or see anything spooky, they at least want someone else to witness it with them.

Strange sounds often come from the Roy Cullen building's second floor. Steve Boss reported that an architect said some eerie noises might come from rafters and old wooden braces in the buildings. Even air pressure in water pipes can be the cause. The architect went out of his way to identify sounds as purely natural—to talk himself into believing it?

Those who do "believe," say ghosts want you to hear only what they want you to hear—or see.

University of Houston
4800 Calhoun Road
Houston, Texas 77004
www.uh.edu.com

A Lofty Place

Two important deaths involving the Rice Hotel could certainly lay the foundation for ghosts. Who doesn't love a murder mystery?

Many men from the east came to Texas for a better life in the nineteenth century. Such was the case with William Marsh Rice, born in 1818, a native of Massachusetts. According to descendant, Archie P. McDonald, Rice first worked in the Milam Hotel's bar in Houston. A poor young man, he moved from New York to seek his fortune. He sought one business venture after another: railroad promoter, investor, cotton ginner, landowner, and hotel owner, all earning him millions.

Although he hadn't yet purchased the land on which the old Capitol of the Republic of Texas stood in Houston, he eventually had it on his "want" list. It was home to the Texas Congress for two years. In 1857, owners of the building sold it for $12,000 to R. S. Blount, who opened the Capitol Hotel on the site.

William Rice, a widower by this time, in 1867 married his second wife, Elizabeth Baldwin Brown, a widow. Rice still had his eye on the hotel. After Colonel A. Groesbeck bought and demolished the Capitol, Rice purchased the property and built a five-story annex. He re-named it the "Rice Hotel."

Realizing he had the money, he was eager to further the educational process in Texas. In 1891, he pushed the charter for the William M. Rice Institute for the Advancement of Literature, Science and Art, incorporated in Austin. He revised his will in 1896 and left the bulk of his estate to his namesake institute, Rice University. Shortly after he signed the new will, Elizabeth died.

The events leading to Rice's death are from what movies are made. According to records in Rice University's Fondren Library, Rice's attorney discovered that Elizabeth had changed her own will to indicate they were both residents of Texas, a community property state.

Elizabeth and William had already agreed their estate would go to the university.

Unknown to William, however, Elizabeth revised her will so that her half of the vast estate, minus only a few thousand dollars, would go to her family members.

Rice's attorney informed him of what his wife had done, and the legal battle began. Elizabeth's executor hired lawyer Albert Patrick to investigate the residency question. At that time, Patrick became acquainted with Rice's valet, Charlie Jones.

Apparently, the ending result favored retaining Rice's will of the estate's beneficiary. So in 1900, Patrick swayed the valet to poison Rice, little by little, with mercury pills. He made up a will with a forged signature, which gave the major portion of Rice's estate to him (Patrick), with only small amounts left to relatives and friends.

The plot thickens. In 1900, the Gulf Coast hurricane severely damaged a refinery William Rice owned. Its manager wired for repair monies that would deplete the current bank account of immediate cash, and Patrick needed that for court defenses. It was then he persuaded Jones to chloroform Rice, since he wasn't dying fast enough. Records state Rice was murdered September 23, 1900.

Hurrying to obtain cash, Patrick used a check Jones had forged. Aha! . . . Jones had misspelled Patrick's name. When the banker called Rice to verify the check, he learned Rice had died. Once the bank contacted Rice's attorney, Captain Baker, suspicions led to an even more sensational trial, which culminated in a guilty verdict for Patrick—sentenced to the electric chair. Even though Jones had done the actual killing, the law released him.

As for Patrick, the governor later commuted his sentence to life, then granted him a full pardon because of errors in "expert testimony" at his murder trial.

So with the lawsuit of residency and the validity of Rice's will finally settled in 1902, Captain Baker and the Board of Trustees continued with Rice's dream of having his money go to the institute of higher learning in Houston.

The main building on this hotel site was demolished, re-built, added to, torn down, and again re-built. It has held Rice's name since 1883. The seventeen-story structure opened on May 17, 1913, at a cost of $2.5 million. It offered the first escalator in a hotel and the state's first public air-conditioned room—the cafeteria—in plenty of time for the Democratic National Convention in 1928.

Six presidents have stayed in the hotel throughout its decades. President John F. Kennedy spoke there before flying to Fort Worth. The President and Mrs. Kennedy spent their last night in the Texas Hotel. After breakfast the following morning, they drove to Fort Worth's Carswell Air Force Base, where they left for that tragic day, November 22, 1963 in Dallas. If his spirit returned to any hotel, it would be the Texas Hotel.

This glamorous Rice Hotel, with all the amenities a guest could desire, closed its doors in 1977. It remained closed for twenty years, but apparently not closed to ghosts.

After a $27.5 million renovation in 1998, the hotel re-opened as "Post Rice Lofts," with spacious apartments showing the advanced popularity of downtown living. The original "Rice Roof" dance pavilion is a

Post Rice Lofts.

residents' social area. The paneled lounge offers a terrace overlooking the city.

Another person of interest in this story is Anson Jones, who also ventured into Texas as a young teenager. He, too, made money and became politically active. He was the last president of the Republic of Texas in 1844. After Sam Houston defeated him as senator to Washington D.C., Jones fell ill to "clinical depression." He fatally shot himself in the hotel on January 9, 1858, at the age of fifty-nine. For years, people have said he returned in spirit form, even after the razing of the first hotel.

Since more than one hotel has stood on this site, that brings up the question: "If a ghost 'existed' in an earlier time in a certain place, does that ghost remain no matter what is currently on the land?" When nothing is on that same land, would the ghost just sit on a tree stump waiting for someone to build something, be it a hotel, house, or whatever, around him? . . . Perhaps no one has brought up that question, but is there an answer?

One resident reported an incident about which she was adamant. While she sat by the swimming pool, she observed a hazy image of a man walking from the far side of the pool. The witness blinked, thinking she was dreaming. As the image came toward her, just before making the turn at the corner of the pool, it vanished.

The pool area is inaccessible to the general public, since the Rice is now a resident hotel.

The "Crystal Ballroom" and lobby of the Rice, now restored, closely resemble the original design of 1913. A bride-to-be and her fiancé were planning their wedding reception soon after the Rice Lofts opened. When they arrived in the ballroom, the lights were dim. They saw the couple waltzing close to the bandstand, then vanish as soon as the lights were turned up. Perhaps they hear music when no one else can.

Another report concerned a young woman wearing a white dress with an organza-ruffled neckline strolling toward the terrace area of the Veranda Club. Attaching names to these apparitions is not that simple. The man in the dark suit could be the ghost of Anson Jones, who committed suicide. Or since William Marsh was particularly

The phantom dancers left before I arrived.

fond of his hotel, he might simply visit on occasion to see how it has progressed to its present state.

As to the single lady . . . Mrs. Anson Jones, perhaps, searching for her husband. And the couple? I have no thought as to their identity, although they *could* be the Rices.

With a history such as this hotel leaves behind—deception, murder, suicide, political controversy, and oh yes, apparitions.

> Post Rice Lofts
> 909 Texas Street
> Houston, Texas 77002
> 713-228-7423

THE SPAGHETTI WAREHOUSE

Let's talk spaghetti. Or ghosts. Or both. Whether or not the building in which you will find terrific Italian food is the most haunted in Texas is debatable. It depends upon whom you ask. There is no doubt about eerie goings-on in the Spaghetti Warehouse on Commerce Street in Houston.

The building was erected in the first decade of the 1900s. Records show it served as a produce warehouse for the Southern Pacific Railroad. Renovated in the 1970s, the Original Spaghetti Warehouse found a home. Antiques are in sight everywhere you look, from an amazing pot-bellied stove, an enormous grandfather clock, to an old trolley car. And oh, yes, a mysterious hutch.

Legend also says an ice-packing plant first occupied the structure and later a pharmaceutical company. While I found no documentation of a pharmaceutical company in Houston during those years, it was possibly a pharmacy, or more likely, called "Druggist."

Let's go with the other legend, the one concerning the produce business, which operated in the 1930s. An elevator ran from the second floor to the basement, a must for transporting loads of vegetables and other perishables stocked there. The temperature stayed relatively cool.

The accepted story tells us the manager of the company fell to his death into the elevator shaft. His wife vowed she saw him arrive home, but the next morning she discovered he wasn't home at all. She hurried to the business to see about him. When she entered the building, a crowd of people stood, whispering and pointing toward the elevator. She

Tell me again how the trolley got on the second floor.

realized the tragic truth when she stared into the elevator shaft and saw her husband, dead. His spirit has made itself known to many people.

The man's widow became a recluse. Exactly one year later, her family went by her house to see her and found her dead. The doctors could find no visible cause of death. Her loved ones felt she died of a broken heart.

Employees say they have seen an apparition of a woman in various places in the restaurant, possibly the woman's image, looking for her husband. A misty outline dressed in white, she floats above the tables, always searching. Staff members believe this doomed man's spirit is still there, particularly inside the elevator and in the basement where the elevator fell.

An almost unbelievable account is someone played "musical chairs" in 1990. According to Jeff Belanger's book, *The World's Most Haunted Places*, and quoting the assistant manager, she made sure everyone was out of the building before she secured the business for the night. When the manager went in to work the next morning, he called her and asked what the deal was with the chairs. She hadn't a clue what he was talking about.

When she went in, almost a hundred dining chairs were stacked to the ceiling. They certainly were not like that when she left the night before. As if it would take a flying Casper to arrange the chairs in such a way, a chair leg of one chair went through the back of the chair just below it, or above, depending on which way you were theorizing, like a puzzle piece. The maze of chairs continued to the ceiling.

Remodeling took place in 1990. Another weird thing happened with the chairs. The crew chief had entered, gone upstairs, then returned when the rest of the crew had not followed him. At that point, he noticed all the chairs were away from the tables. When he closed the door, it accidentally locked the crew outside. By that time, with such an eerie happening, they all left in a rush.

The Spaghetti Warehouse employees have experiences of the ghostly kind. They've heard whispers, particularly when an individual is alone in the basement. They've also felt cold slaps of air. From time to time, objects would be in places they were not in originally.

Pete Haviland and his team have visited the Spaghetti Warehouse a number of times, even spending the night on one occasion. During the course of these investigations, they came away with shots of paranormal anomalies, such as one photograph with mist in the elevator, vortexes, significant EMF spikes.

Pete observed the apparition of a little girl standing in the corner of an upstairs room. A photograph, while not showing the child, contained a clear orb. The group has no doubt that something very paranormal continues to live in the Spaghetti Warehouse, just as people have reported for decades.

One of the most unusual segments of the haunting is based around an antique hutch with an urn painted on the front. It once belonged to a family who had nine children, all dying before the age of 12. The hutch once held urns with the ashes of the children. As the assistant manager said, "A portable cemetery."

Pete invited two psychics to his investigations of the restaurant. Each sensed that a small girl had once played hide-in-seek in the hutch. Somehow she became locked inside and suffocated. One of the psychics said she heard the faint sound of a child crying, coming from the hutch.

People have reported seeing the form of a little girl in front of a large grandfather clock, which stands on the first floor. The same child? And perhaps the one Pete observed standing in the corner? And the one he saw playing with a ball?

The manager said she saw four translucent spirits float by in front of her. No one has volunteered to work alone in the building at night since that time. That spirits floating thing can be downright intimidating.

The Spaghetti Warehouse
901 Commerce Street
Houston, Texas 77002
713-229-8504
www.meatballs.com

LA CARAFE

Act I: "La Carafe" could be the title of a Broadway show. This bar is one of the most fascinating wine bars in the country. The 130-year-old building needs a little back-story.

A not-at-all-shy woman, Pamela Mann, migrated from New York to Houston in the 1830s.

Rumor has it that New York either escorted her out of town, or she decided to leave on her own. A second rumor indicated she had killed a rival, possibly by accident. So, either way, leaving town was her best choice. Pamela was a prostitute. Moving to Houston did not change her profession. She came to town with a bang.

Pamela, one of the early settlers of Harris County, obviously arrived in Houston with a tidy sum of money, because she opened up the Mansion House Hotel at the corner of Congress and Milam Streets. It became a well-known boisterous place, complete with fights, an assortment of tempting females on the second floor—and police raids.

She purchased almost an entire block, bought other property and had her own yoke of oxen. Somehow Sam Houston met up with her. He desperately needed her oxen to pull his "Twin Sisters," or canons, as far as Nacogdoches, where he would return them. Thing was, he apparently wasn't going on to Nacogdoches. History tells us when she realized he had turned toward San Jacinto, she pulled out her pistols—twin pistols—and called him a liar. With that threat, she had no problem bringing her oxen back to Houston.

Opposite page:
The mystifying painted hutch.

Pamela had a certain charisma, aside from the twins, so much so that when she received a death sentence for forgery in 1839 (not her only crime), Mirabeau Lamar, president of the Republic of Texas, pardoned her.

She enjoyed a short-lived freedom, as she died in a yellow fever epidemic of the early 1840s. Interestingly, for a woman in her profession, Pamela Mann collected four husbands, the last having passed away only a few months before Pamela died.

Act II of "La Carafe" opens with John Kennedy, an Irish immigrant born in 1819 and purchasing the property in the 1840s. Since he was a baker by trade, he opened a bakery in a portion of the building in which the Mansion House had been years before. He traded with the Indians and made his mark as a respected businessman. His being in the right place at the wrong time caused his demise. While Kennedy stood outside his business, someone shot him dead.

Fire destroyed this two-story brick building, but the current structure still stands on the original foundation. The National Register for Historic Places has it listed; it is also reportedly the oldest bar in Houston. The building has been home to a pony express office, pharmacy, barbershop and a dry goods store. In 1954, it stood vacant. In 1958, "McReynolds Assocs." occupied the premises, then left it vacant another two years.

The National Register notes that after five generations, the Kennedy family agreed to sell it to William V. Berry, who operated it in 1970. All those years open up the possibility for numerous hauntings. Since Pamela Mann was an early owner of the building, she would have first anomaly rights to visit.

Act III: Bring on the Ghosts. Footsteps sound from upstairs. The second floor is sometimes used for storage, although it is set up for customers when necessary. Bartenders, regular staff, waiters, and customers tend to agree strange noises come from the stairs and the floor above. When people have gone to investigate, all sounds stop, and certainly no human is there. EMF meters gauge an unearthly presence, as they often spike.

Members of HoustonSeance.com, wrote that people have reported sounds of children playing on the second floor. This apparently comes from the story of a fire, which took the lives of several children.

As Pete Haviland said, the bar manager once related to him that when he closed for the night, he felt that someone watched him on the way to his car. He turned back to see somebody peering out a second floor window. But when he returned inside, no one was there. Makes it a little eerie to work alone at night.

Where spirits sometimes dwell.

With various occupants for so many decades, just who are the ghosts? La Carafe is a living legend—just not all living. Carved initials and names cover the heavy wooden bar's surface. Pictures line the walls, those of regular customers as well as celebrities. The place is low-lit, intimate, and loaded with atmosphere. Those who are sensitive to the paranormal have felt the presence of spirits throughout the bar.

Accidents have occurred on the stairs at La Carafe. True, accidents can happen at any time on stairways, but since the bar does have a haunted reputation, who is to say spirits didn't cause the people to trip? That's paranormal spirits, but you knew that.

The woman who is most seen is identified as Pamela Mann. The apparition wanders around the tables, then "whoosh," she is up the stairs.

And back to John Kennedy, the former owner of the property. Guests reported more than once of seeing an apparition dressed in dark

Beware the stairs.

clothing. Of course, the apparition doesn't have to be John Kennedy. It could be anyone of many past owners or customers. During the 1950s and 60s when the structure stood vacant, apparitions of ghosts past must have enjoyed private time in a vacant building. When the bar opened, the ghosts still felt they had the float of the place.

The owner has owned the bar since 1987, serving from a lengthy list of wine and beer. Be sure to bring cash. As if ghosts might sign their receipts with disappearing ink, to be fair, they don't accept credit cards from anyone.

If you're immune to the cold pricklies, schedule an evening at this historical bar, even stay for a late-night séance. Don't mind the eerie hand that might rest on your shoulder. It may be a ghost from the past wanting to join you in a cool one.

Still, if you're a bit nervous in La Carafe, remember . . . you'll never walk alone.

La Carafe
813 Congress Street
Houston, Texas 77002
713-229-9399
www.owlnet.rice.edu/~hans320/projects/lacarafe/

JEFFERSON DAVIS HOSPITAL

Two Jefferson hospitals once existed at the same time in Houston, but one is now known as the Elder Street Artists Lofts. The city purchased the five acres from the Allen brothers in 1840. The land was home to a graveyard.

This "City Cemetery," segregated in sections, included Masons, Odd Fellows, suicides, gunfighters, and general undesirables. Victims of the 1867 yellow fever epidemic shared a mass grave. A large percentage of the corpses were soldiers, mostly Confederates, but many of the Union Army. And while we're allotting percentages, a certain amount goes for spirits of any, or many, of the above.

The total estimate buried there is between 5,000 and 10,000. According to George Wolf Jr.'s article in *Old Cemeteries of Harris Co., Texas*, the last burial was in 1904. Death's requirements surpassed the space in the old graveyard.

Now enters the excavation for the first Jefferson Davis Hospital in 1924, on one large portion of the cemetery. Wolf quotes a woman as having said, "They are out there digging up people . . . and just throwing the bones out!" A man recalled, after witnessing the proceedings, "They were putting bones in nail kegs or crates." Without any proof of reburial, no one knows for certain what became of all those bones. Records show that the Odd Fellows never used their section, and after learning of the plans for the hospital, the Masons immediately exhumed their dead.

A member of the Super family didn't take kindly to the disruption of his family's burial places. The man stood with a shotgun on the site, daring construction workers or anyone else to disturb them. He stood his ground all right, because the graves still remain. They have a coverlet of green grass and flowers, with original concrete borders near the building's entrance.

The structure had three stories and an above-ground basement, erected to avoid disturbing the graves below. With a large edifice sitting on a cemetery, that's ghostrophobia in the truest sense. Dirt covering a grave is acceptable, but at least a view of blue sky is above, not the same as the underside of a brick building.

With the completion of the first hospital, the country praised it as one of the most modern in the United States. After gaining such an outstanding reputation, it soon exceeded capacity. Fourteen years after its construction in 1924, a second hospital carrying the same name but with 11 stories and 500 beds, replaced it.

In 1968, the Houston Fire Department built a maintenance facility on the remaining portion of the land, destroying many graves. Some people believe the destruction of gravesites frees the spirits who are buried there, but only those who have not crossed over to the other side.

The city excavated a utility trench in 1986, unearthing around thirty more burial sites. Since graveyards are under the protection of Texas Law, officials called in Dr. Kenneth Brown of the Department of Anthropology at the University of Houston. Everyone thought it was the site of the old city cemetery, but Dr. Brown questioned it because of the bodies buried in fresh black earth and leaves—"black earth graves."

Brown was familiar with this custom from his research in England as well as in the Carolinas. Soil covering the bodies was of a high organic nature, which aided in decomposition; therefore, black earth graves. The English used the practice mainly because they thought fumes of plague victims could spread the disease.

The bones now lie, along with the thirty-two unknown Confederate soldiers, on the site of the Houston Fire Department. The grave marker honoring the soldiers in 1897, is still there.

Some archeologists believed the first planned cemetery rests over a pre-existing graveyard. After the excavation of about forty of these graves, they discovered bodies wrapped in shrouds, with no coffins.

Archeologists also discovered ceramic pieces dating from the seventeenth century. Since English colonists used these types of ceramics, Brown felt they were the earliest settlers (besides Indians) in this Texas area. In essence, the Jefferson Davis Hospital was on top of an English colony of the 1600s.

The "new" Jefferson Davis, built in 1937 and located on the south bank of Buffalo Bayou and Allen Parkway, had no intensive care unit. Patients received treatment in only two rooms. It was a larger facility, but lack of funding and the inability to provide for victims of train wrecks and car crashes, it couldn't meet the need of trauma victims. The city demolished it in 1999.

Abandoned for twenty years, the Elder Street address became a source for graffiti, beer cans, vagrants, and break-ins. It is here some believe those buried beneath its soil will not rest.

The beliefs have triggered the interest of many who want to see for themselves. Employees during the active years reported apparitions, shadows, and voices coming from patients' empty rooms. We can speculate as to who the mysterious shadows were. Were they reflections of those who died as patients, or impatient souls still buried beneath?

At one time, the old hospital was a rehab center, then later used for storage, including equipment and archival papers, some of which have disappeared. During the time of storage, reports of eerie experiences drifted about. Such an experience occurred when more than one person professed to smelling various medicinal solutions. The odor was particularly prevalent on the top floor, where the operating rooms were. This locale also housed the children's ward, which opened to the rooftop garden and play area.

On another occasion, when three young people slipped in and ventured to the fourth floor, they saw what they believed to be a nurse. She stopped, looked at them with a sympathetic expression, turned back the way she came and vanished. This so unnerved the boys, they raced to the rooftop and clamored down the outside wall to a window below. Climbing in, they exited through a lower floor's broken window, the same way they had entered, their only choice if they wanted to avoid running into the ghost again.

As reported on *ABC Eyewitness News Houston*, August 1, 2003, Andy Cerota wrote about a group of college kids who decided to go on a ghost hunt. They chose Jefferson Davis Hospital. The boys had heard of others who had seen "all sorts of crazy stuff" there. The idea sounded good, so they arrived after one o'clock in the morning to see for themselves. It was a little spookier than they thought it would be, but they were all set for any ghost that might pop up. Besides, they'd have a good story to tell their friends.

Another participant in the ghost-busting project said the rest were in front of him when he heard what sounded like a "cap gun." At first, he stopped in his tracks, listening. He thought it was maybe a rat bumping over a soda can. Then he heard the sound again, closer. When he saw a bullet ricochet in front of him, he realized it was for real.

It wasn't a ghost who fired the shot. The boys gave up their keys, wallets, and cell phones to the robber who shot at them. Police soon surrounded the building, thinking the K-9s could track down the suspects. But they had disappeared before the police arrived.

In addition to losing their valuables, the young men probably lost their desire to go ghost chasing, at least, for a while.

The city fathers, as well as citizens, grew disgruntled at seeing the abandoned hospital with its landscape of weeds and dead grass. They considered tearing it down. But there were those who saw the once impressive old building as something worth saving. Different groups offered suggestions: Do away with it and leave it as an open field or a park. Have high-priced apartments. No, low-income housing. Better still, a museum.

Ultimately, with a lot of hard work, in September 2004, the Avenue Community Development Corporation and Artspace Projects began renovating the old hospital into the Elder Street Artists Lofts.

The days of chasing ghosts in the dark of night are over, unless of course, you lease a loft there. It is hoped a residing artist with paintbrush in hand, will capture a likeness of any apparitions of early English settlers, soldiers, or whoever might appear roaming through the halls.

What of those feeling an ethereal presence, or of seeing shadowy figures? Tenants will get used to it. Ye olde Jefferson Hospital is now an attractive brought-back-to-glory residential development, a place where any resident revenant would be proud.

Elder Street Artists Lofts
1101 Elder Street
Houston, Texas 77007
713-223-2787

Elder Street Artists Lofts (from story on opposite page).

JUDGE FOR YOURSELF

Judge Woodrow Bradley Seals isn't the only judge whose spirit seems to return to his courtroom. Judge Roy Bean, for instance, still returns to sit in his rocking chair on the porch of the Jersey Lily Saloon in Langtry. He might even pour a shot for you from behind the bar. But Judge Seals made his mark in history a hundred years later and is apparently responsible for the ghostly activity in his old courtroom.

When a legend is attached to a specific person, it's helpful to try to figure out why this particular individual either chooses not to cross over, or simply returns at various times, according to his or her desires. Spirits can do that, you know.

Judge Seals was born in Bogalusa, Louisiana, on December 24, 1917. During World War II, he was a pilot, retiring as Lieutenant Colonel in the Air Force Reserve. In 1949, he received his Doctorate from The University of Texas School of Law.

With degree in hand, he and his family moved to Houston, where he began his law practice. He didn't sit around and wait for things to happen. He made them happen. Judge Seals was a religious man, and in the Methodist Church, he founded the Society of St. Stephen, a national program aimed at helping people in need. He served as John F. Kennedy's presidential campaign manager in 1960. As United States Attorney for the Southern District, he hired the first African-American secretary in a U.S. Attorney's Office in Texas. The list goes on and on.

Among his honors were the Papal Medal "Benerementi" (not normally bestowed upon a non-Catholic) from Pope John Paul II. He also received the Medal of Honor from the Daughters of the American Revolution, as well as the World Methodist Council Peace Award, in 1987.

Judge Seals's courtroom was on the tenth floor of Houston's Ben Casey Federal Court Building. The building was never known as haunted, except for the hall leading to the courtroom and the room itself.

The spacious law library serves attorneys and judges. Courtrooms were all in use the day I went there, including that of Judge Seals. If his spirit does indeed return to his courtroom, he probably visits the library to catch up on current cases.

The judge smoked cigars in life, and the aroma of cigar smoke drifts in and out the courtroom, although nobody is smoking. When a person walks down the hall toward the judge's chambers, it's as if someone is accompanying them to the doorway to escort them in. Employees of the cleaning crew have commented on hearing whispers as they do their evening's work. And security guards have wondered just how far security reaches.

Of course, Enron "went down" on the ninth floor. Did residual energy rise? Judge Seals always preferred his chambers to be colder than usual, which people say it now is. Or, the judge may be paying a visit, bringing with him a drop in temperature.

Judge Seals died in 1990 after open-heart surgery. It all fits. With legends as they are, and with an impressive lifetime such as Judge Seals led, why wouldn't he want to return now and then, to "his" courtroom?

Bob Casey Federal Building
515 Rusk
Houston, Texas 77002

The Library of the Federal Building (from story on opposite page).

THE ESPERSON BUILDING

The Esperson Building in Houston is mindful of the Mausolus Tomb of ancient Greek's city of Halicarnassus in 377 B.C.

Kansas-born Mellie Keenan moved to Oklahoma with her mother and stepfather. While there, she met and fell in love with Niels Esperson, of Denmark. When he first came to America, he purchased a dictionary for $30 out of his annual salary of $130, so he could teach himself English. The couple married in 1893 and soon moved to Houston.

Mellie was no stay-at-home wife, not with her spirit of motivation. She set about to learn intricate dealings concerning oil, so the *Handbook of Texas* tells us. Niels, a developer of the oil business, and his wife, became millionaires in oil, real estate, and other business ventures.

Niels died in 1922, leaving his widow significant wealth from an oil-rich ranch to a tile plant in Kansas. Her first venture into construction was to hire America's greatest cinema architect, John Eberson, to design and build the Majestic Theatre, now demolished.

Before Niels died, he visualized a superlative downtown office building. Mellie didn't know exactly what her husband pictured, but she knew she wanted it to be great—nothing Houston had seen before. She traveled to Europe, absorbing ideas, materials, architecture, for such a project. Upon her return, she again hired Eberson, known as the "Valentino of Cinema Design," to bring her dream to fulfillment—a memorial to her late husband.

The thirty-two story Italian Renaissance building is indeed a fitting memorial. For romantics, this tribute to her husband joins the story of Mausolus. With his queen Artemisia, he ruled over Halicarnassus for 24 years. When he died, he left his wife (also his sister) heartbroken—it was the custom for rulers to marry their sisters. In his memory, she built the most magnificent tomb, one of the Seven Wonders of the Ancient World.

That probably has nothing to do with the ghosts of the Esperson Building, but the comparison was hard to resist. The building features a gold-leaf tower, urns, sculpture, obelisks—everything an Art Deco building might have. It's all there—just too far away to see from the sidewalk.

As to the rumor someone is buried on top of the building? Not true, according to Houstonist.com. So, the building's dome does indeed resemble a tomb, giving credence to the rumor. Some have assumed Niels himself rested there. No; the couple was buried in Forest Park Lawndale Cemetery. And the dome area is closed to the public, although in the early days, visitors could sit at a table and dine. It is no longer an observation deck.

Again turning to her favored architect, Mellie had him design a smaller adjoining structure, named for her. It is basically a separate building, although most floors join.

It was common knowledge, from the various organizations and philanthropies in which Mellie was involved, she held Houston close to her heart. Her own office was on the twenty-fifth floor of "her" building, where she worked until losing her eyesight, dying in 1945. It is no wonder Mellie would be considered the source of paranormal anomalies. One courier who frequented the elevator commented that she always felt chilled. Especially when in the lift alone, she sensed she wasn't alone at all.

Opposite page:
Hers and His

One person who formerly worked in the lower "tunnel system" of the building reported having recurring electrical problems in their suite.

The doors would lock, and particularly when major reconstruction took place on the street level above the suites, it seemed someone else was in the office. Items were moved, and the employee called management to change the side door lock, as well as that on the exit door. Still, the mysterious occurrences continued.

If anything needed to be changed in Mellie Esperson's building, we can be certain she wanted to oversee it. In 2004 *The Houston Chronicle* reported the sale of the Espersons' buildings for $48 million. Mellie and Niels would be proud.

The Esperson Building
808 Travis Street
Houston, Texas 77002
713-224-1663
www.espersonbuildings.com

NIGHT MUSIC

Click . . . click . . . click. The ghost of Pete, a large German Shepherd returns to keep watch when the library is ready to close. The crisp sounds of his toenails on the hard surface floors warn patrons it's time to leave. And what of the music? Who is responsible for the melodious strains of a violin?

The personnel expect patrons to remain reasonably quiet. In past years, even as much as a sneeze brought about the wraith, er, wrath of the staff member on duty. It appears absolute quiet doesn't apply to ghosts, at least not when it's going-home-time in downtown Houston's Julia Bedford Ideson Library.

Julia Ideson moved with her family from Nebraska to Houston in 1891. As a teenager, she entered the University of Texas as a student of its first library science class. After graduation in 1903, her first job was being in charge of the Houston Lyceum Library.

As in many cities, Andrew Carnegie presented a monetary gift for establishing a "palace of books," if the city provided additional funds. His $50,000 made Julia's dream come true. In 1926, a new central library replaced the Lyceum at Smith and McKinney. When still the head of the Houston system, she directed the opening of six branches. It seemed fitting after her death in 1945 that one of them would be renamed in her honor.

The caretaker or night watchman, J. Frank Cramer, lived in an apartment in the basement.

He owned a German Shepherd named Pete. His dog accompanied him in the corridors, helping check to see if all remained in order for the night.

The watchman spent many evenings playing his violin. This was usually after patrons had gone home. If he finished his daily work schedule, he would pick up the instrument to practice. Patrons could hear the sound of a violin filtering from the basement. Witnesses say he preferred Strauss waltzes.

At night you can sometimes hear violin music.

Cramer joined the staff in 1926 and served it well until his death ten years later. One day he complained of chest pains. The staff reacted immediately and rushed him to the hospital where he soon died. Who took care of his dog? We can surmise either his family or Julia Ideson saw to Pete's well being.

At one time, Cramer had planted a tree outside near the entry. No one is certain, but the belief is his dog grieved himself to death under this shade tree. But I believe Pete is again happy, walking by his master's side.

Soon after the custodian died, reports of violin music being heard spread throughout the building. Not only have people heard the beautiful music, they have detected the sound of Pete's toenails echoing on the floors.

According to Michele Moore, General Manager of Houston's High Spirits Tours, J. Frank Cramer's sister arrived from Manhattan, Kansas, to transfer her brother's remains back home.

By 1971, the city had outgrown the Ideson Library. Because it held such a meaningful place in Houston's past, the city fathers did not have it demolished. Instead, they restored it after the construction of a new central library next door. It seems fitting that special research collections and information concerning Houston have a home in Julia Ideson's "House of Knowledge."

The library's new archival wing as on the original blueprints of 1926 began in January 2009. The Great Depression ceased construction of this valuable extension of the building. The expansion will be the repository for historic Houston photographs, rare books and more than 300 rare maps of the Southwest dating from 1561, and will provide space, humidity, and climate control.

As for the violin music, the fact is, those who walk outside, or staff members who work late, sometime hear night music. From 1936 until her death in 1945, Julia Ideson could take pleasure in the lilting melody of Strauss's "By the Beautiful Blue Danube."

Julie Ideson Library
500 McKinney
Houston, Texas 77002
713-236-1313
www.hpl.lib.tx.us

Listen for the German Shepherd's click, click on the tiles.

GHOST LIGHT

Viewing the exterior of Houston's Alley Theatre takes you right to Broadway. And on the inside, you feel you're really there.

A theatre ghost is not exactly new to anyone. The reason why a ghost haunts a place holds our fascination. People believe Iris Siff's spirit is still in the theatre she loved.

In 1947, Nina Vance and Mr. and Mrs. Robert Altfeld founded the amateur acting group. With its beginning in a small eighty-five-seat theatre, it grew to one of the most esteemed resident theatres in the United States. It moved in 1949 to an abandoned fan factory at the end of an alley; therefore, its name.

The Alley became fully professional in 1954 in a new location, with a resident company. To offset financial difficulties, Nina Vance hired stars to bring in the crowds. Her idea worked beautifully. Before

long, the operation received grants allowing them to construct a new complex with two theatres, one seating 824 with a thrust stage, and another, a 296-seat arena stage.

The Alley's first world premiere, *The Effect of Gamma Rays on Man-in-the-Moon Marigolds* later won a Pulitzer Prize on Broadway. In 1996, the Alley received the Regional Theatre Tony Award.

A most interesting incident occurred when Michael Moriarty of *Law and Order* suddenly stopped in the middle of a play in the 1970s. According to Houston.citysearch.com, Moriarty said he was "too tired to continue and walked off the stage." He also left town.

Enter Iris Siff, one of the most influential women of theatre in the Southwest. A native Oklahoman, she graduated with a degree in theatre from the University of Texas. Her early career was as a radio field representative to South America. She joined the Alley as an actress a year after its inception and soon became assistant to Nina Vance.

In 1971, she approached Mel Dacus, managing director of Casa Manana in Fort Worth, with the proposal of forming a theatrical school for children. For $2,000, Casa accepted the offer, and Mrs. Siff incorporated the "Merry-Go-Round" school. The name later changed to the Casa Manana Playhouse, to attract students of all ages. I was a member of the staff of drama instructors and recall Iris as a friend and a woman devoted to the theatre. She never considered it work. It was a passion.

After Vance's death in 1980, Mrs. Siff took over as managing director and formed the Alley Academy and the Studio School of Theatre.

The Texas theatre world suffered, when, two years after Mrs. Siff accepted control of the Alley, she met her death in her office early on January 13, 1982. No one could verify whether or not she had worked late on the 12th, or arrived very early on Wednesday, the 13th. It didn't matter. She was filling out an application for a government grant. What Mrs. Siff did not know was Clifford X. Phillips, a former security guard, whom she had fired a few weeks before, was in the building. Familiar with the layout, he reportedly came to her office with robbery on his mind—not expecting anyone to be there. An argument ensued and Phillips, a.k.a. Abdullah Bashir, strangled her with a telephone cord.

Authorities found him at his mother's Los Angeles home, where he readily confessed to the murder. He received the death penalty by lethal injection, carried out December 15, 1993 in Huntsville. A witness quoted him as expressing remorse. According to public records, Phillips's death statement included, "Certainly murder cannot be an instrument of Allah."

The legend is, the ghost of Iris Siff remains in the Alley Theatre. Actors not even born at the time of her murder have sensed her presence. If, indeed, a performer is more motivated during a particular scene, he can credit the spirit of Iris Siff.

Expect to see her image sitting in a front row seat. The ghost light in the Alley Theatre may never go out.

The Alley Theatre
615 Texas Street
Houston, Texas 77002
713-220-5700
www.alleytheatre.org

La Porte

La Porte is twenty-five miles east of Houston on Galveston Bay. Considered a "new" city, a group of men founded it as a business venture in 1892. Records don't show why I. R. Holmes, T. W. Lee, A. M. and J. H. York named it La Porte, French for *the door*, but it's been La Porte for over 115 years, so apparently no one objected.

Bishop Nicholas A. Gallagher founded St. Mary's Seminary in 1900, when the town had a little over 500 residents. The seminary moved to Houston in 1954. Certainly, this entire area of Texas was subject to hurricanes, and La Porte was not left out. In 1915, just before World War I, a fire destroyed most of the business district and a tumultuous hurricane damaged even more.

The Sylvan Beach Amusement Park of the 20s and 30s created a welcomed economy to the town. Top big bands, including Benny Goodman and Phil Harris performed, especially during the summer. Beauty contests added to the entertainment.

Even though the population was never so great, the Lyndon B. Johnson Space Center and Bayport Channel aided the city's prosperity, and people moved in. And consider the La Porte-Baytown Tunnel, which opened in 1954. It was quite an addition to a small town.

Because of the larger ships being channeled through, the tunnel had to be removed. The longest cable-stayed bridge in Texas took its place—the Fred Hartman Bridge, eight football fields long.

A small town grew, both in population and prestige. The Battle of San Jacinto was fought on this site, attested to with a National Historic Landmark status, brought about by the Texas Parks and Wildlife Department, and consists of the Monument, Battleground, and the once "most powerful weapon in the world, Battleship Texas."

BATTLESHIP TEXAS

If reports are true, the Battleship Texas is the only haunted battleship in the world—above water. As a weapon, it was once the most powerful in the world. Commissioned in 1914, it was not only the most powerful but the largest—the only vessel that served in World War I, as well as World War II.

Battleship Texas saw duty in Iwo Jima and Okinawa, Normandy, North Africa, and France. It fired on the Nazis on D-Day. To pay back, German artillery hit the ship near Cherbourg, France, but it weathered that storm. The battleship became the first memorial museum in the United States in 1944.

According to *Texas Wildlife and Parks*, "'The Texas' was presented to the State of Texas and commissioned as the flagship of the Texas Navy. In 1983, the ship was placed under the stewardship of the Texas Parks and Wildlife Department and is permanently anchored on the Buffalo Bayou and the busy Houston Ship Channel."

Art Chapman reported in his December 6, 2006 column of the *Fort Worth Star-Telegram* that "millions of federal dollars had been earmarked to begin its rehabilitation—has disappeared." The $16 million has gone. "In the blink of an eye the Federal Highway Administration started a deadly domino effect by asking the Texas Department of Transportation to withhold $350 million in federal funds."

Federal authorities have announced the money was needed for Hurricane Katrina damage, as well as to continue the war on terrorism. The Legislature also approved more than $12 million in bonds to pay for renovations several years ago. They never appropriated the funds.

The great news in 2008 is that on November 6, 2007, voters approved (proposition 4) to allocate $25 million to dry-berth the Battleship Texas for long-term preservation. Donations and volunteers are still needed. Visit the Website, www.battleshiptexas.org.

Now about these ghosts aboard the Battleship Texas. A recurring report concerns a sailor who has attained the name, "Red." He's never introduced himself, but having red hair made the name appropriate. Red apparently wanders the decks. Someone specifically sited him smiling and standing by a ladder, so Jim Parsons, staff writer for the *Daily Cougar* wrote it in a feature article.

Parsons also noted that a caretaker in the trophy room, which is on the same deck, stepped into the room, viewing a bizarre residual image of a Normandy cemetery. Her experience could be a space-time warp. It was disturbing and very real. The room is for displaying guns, various military equipment, photographs and other memorabilia.

Its connection with the cemetery is the fact the Battleship Texas participated in the invasion at Normandy. This was a most unusual experience in residual haunting, a moment in time, which is imprinted in the environment.

The Texas instituted a "sleepover" program open to organized youth groups, ages 7-18. They can sleep in the same 4-tier bunk quarters as the crew. They will tour sections of the ship that are not available to regular tour visitors. This includes having their meals as sailors of fifty years ago did, as well as to perform some of the same duties.

Another report (Citysearch) from a young woman who toured the battleship, concerned her having seen several men "bustling about." She viewed one man in particular, whose image was very clear. He made eye contact. Of perhaps Italian descent, the man dressed informally—"dark pants, undershirt and a Dixie Cup cap." He was brunette, "had dark eyes and heavy eyebrows." He appeared to be in his "mid-20's, with a heavy 5 o'clock shadow."

What comes tomorrow will one day be history, but today, tour this grand vessel for the history most of us have never seen before. Students and visitors can reach out and touch their heritage . . . and maybe a red-haired sailor.

> Battleship Texas
> 3523 Highway 134
> La Porte, Texas 77571
> 281-479-2431

COLUMBUS

Where Columbus is now, an Indian village once stood, known on early maps as "Montezuma." In 1823, Stephen F. Austin settled it as Beason's Ferry. He put out great effort collecting survey fees from his colonists during the Frontier life of the Runaway Scrape. The village received the name, Columbus, in 1835, when Texas was on the edge of rebellion.

General Sam Houston torched it to the ground during his retreat in the Texas Revolution in order to divert the Mexican Army. He was then triumphant in the decisive battle at San Jacinto, which won Texas's Independence.

Approximate population of Columbus is 4,000. You'll find the Turner-Chapman Gallery, owned by world-renowned artist Kenneth Turner and philanthropist, Mark Chapman. The town is fortunate to have the Nesbitt Memorial Library, which hosts lectures, musical performances by world-famous musicians, as well as author lectures and book signings. And not to forget, the 1900's art-deco, Tiffany-style glass dome in the Colorado County Courthouse.

This is a small town with big city offerings.

"LIVE OAKS, AND DEAD FOLKS"

Old City Cemetery in Columbus is a very old burial ground, with many yellow fever victims and Confederate soldiers calling it home. Impressive monuments grace its grounds.

Leisurely walking through it brings visuals of those who were once "live folks."

The Nesbitt Memorial Library conducts cemetery tours, "Live Oaks, and Dead Folks," during an annual Fall weekend. Actors in period costumes step from behind various tombstones and tell stories about former citizens buried there. They offer the same tour at Odd Fellows Cemetery.

While Bob Stafford rests (or does he?) along with other Staffords in the Odd Fellows Cemetery, it's the Old City Cemetery, which holds the most paranormal activity. Even if no vortex or orbs show up on film, just being there makes the hair on your arms stand at attention.

The interred do not have to be famous—all things being equal—they're dead.

The flood of 1913 washed away many headstones, leaving no identification as to who rests where. Records account for some burials and genealogical research serves as proof for others. The city estimates around 500 graves are unmarked. During many years, sunken areas have made it easier to estimate the number.

One grave in particular may cause anomalies and other ethereal disturbances. It's that of John W. Sargent, assumed secretary of the renowned magician, Houdini. In 1929, the same year Houdini died, a three-car accident near Columbus resulted in the death of two men. One, identified as John W. Sargent, had a diary in his possession, indicating he had traveled extensively. The family requested his burial as a pauper.

Five years after, when a similar accident left an unidentified young man dead, local folks recalled the story of Houdini's assumed secretary. According to the *Colorado Country Citizen*, in the 1930s, more than one person recalled a man with that name as having worked with Howard Carter when he opened King Tut's tomb. The superstition was that anyone desecrating an Egyptian grave would suffer a violent death. H. R. Sargent's traveling companion at the time, confirmed he was at King Tut's tomb in 1922. That could account for Sargent's travel shown in his diary.

Mandy and Ralph Prater, my friends who later visited the Stafford Opera House also strolled through Old City Cemetery. Mandy is more sensitive to the paranormal than her husband, who hasn't fully accepted such things as ghosts, although he admits to showing more interest than he formerly did.

This time, he was in agreement. The days had grown shorter, and it was twilight. They had walked near the middle of the graveyard when dozens of minute lights swayed and shifted in bunches, as if strung on a fragile net. Then the anomaly vanished. They thought, but only for a moment, that it was a reflection from automobiles. Quickly, the lights returned, pulsating back and forth.

Fireflies aren't around like they used to be many years ago, and the Praters dismissed that idea. Having witnessed enough, they returned to their car, still remembering the beauty of the cemetery but also carrying with them the eerie feeling they had of the twinkling lights, each no bigger than the head of a pin.

So I'll leave Old City Cemetery with that and wonder if indeed, John W. Sargent is still traveling in the living world.

Old City Cemetery
1300 Block of Walnut Street
Columbus, Texas 78934
For information, call Nesbitt Memorial Library:
979-732-3392

GRAND OPERA

To begin with, I figured the Stafford Opera House was in Stafford, inside the boundary of my proposed itinerary. After realizing it was actually farther west, also in Columbus, I was too involved in the story to give up. I had heard about the opera phantom and wanted to see for myself.

The Galveston, Harrisburg, and San Antonio Railway came into Columbus, providing prosperity, except for one thing. Just prior to the Civil War, R. E. Stafford, known as "Bob," arrived from Georgia and plunged into the cattle business. He drove his cattle north rather than use the rails; thereby, beginning his considerable fortune. The railway didn't get his business. Industrious as he was, he built the Columbus Meatpacking Plant and shipped dressed beef all over the United States and to Havana, Cuba. Several of Bob's brothers and sisters and other family members joined him after the Civil War.

Bob had the beginnings of an empire and added to it by commissioning renowned architect Richard Layton to design an opera house in 1886. The building was also home to Stafford's private bank and a general store on the first floor, with the opera house on the second. It was not the kind we know today, with sloping floors and balconies. But it boasted the largest flat-floored opera house in Texas, with 1,000 chairs and gas-burning chandeliers.

The same year, Stafford had his own house built right next door. He designed it so he could look out his bedroom window and see the stage performances. The grand opening was *As in a Looking Glass*, starring the fabulous Lillian Russell. Harry Houdini was another prominent entertainer, performing to sold-out audiences. People rode the trains from distant towns to attend the shows.

The town needed a new courthouse, the start date being delayed until the locals agreed on who would manufacture the bricks. With the eventual completion of the courthouse, 3,000 county citizens gathered for a barbecue on the 4th of July, 1890. Afterward, they planned to attend Bob Stafford's party at the opera house, during which time they would lay the building's cornerstone.

Even with all the prosperity, a feud had developed among the Staffords and the Townsends—one of those feuds about which no one knew the real cause. The Staffords refused to be crossed, and with cattle rustling rampant, one brother met his death and another, wounded.

An hour before the party, a disagreement ensued between Bob Stafford and his brother John, with City Marshall Larkin Hope, son-in-law of Sheriff Townsend joining in. In the heat of the disagreement, Larkin and his brother Marion shot and killed Bob and John Stafford.

After Bob's death, good fortune in Columbus waned for years to come. The meatpacking plant closed, as did the opera house and other of Bob Stafford's endeavors. Little of the Stafford fortune remained in Columbus. With no one punished for the killings, outrage persisted.

Several gunfights continued, with more murders to follow, revenge for what many thought was a pre-meditated murder of Bob Stafford. The town even unincorporated until 1927. The theatre closed for several years, and other businesses occupied the building. During that time, the second floor opened as a roller rink.

Justice more or less prevailed when Townsend died in 1894. Larkin Hope ran for office, but someone murdered him before the election. The man who took over was voted out, then killed in a downtown gun battle. More murders followed. Travelers bypassed this little town known as "Hells Half Acre."

Theatrical productions resumed in 1991. A dinner theatre offers performances from October to June. Round tables for six or eight can accommodate 300 people for this entertainment by professional actors.

Unquestionably, a manifestation has presented itself to more than one member of the audience. One of the theatre staff told me that a "lady in gray" has drifted in and out, never remaining more than a few seconds. No one can imagine who she is. Lillian Russell making a return engagement? Nevertheless, she meanders through the theatre area, as if a gossamer mist.

There is also a definite masculine spirit, as reported by Ralph and Mandy Prater. They each felt it, as well as smelling cigar smoke, the latter a recognized indication of a spirit. The same sensation followed them upstairs to the theatre. Of course, city ordinance does not allow smoking. As they walked up the steps, a little late for the social hour that precedes dinner, a rapidly moving haze passed by in front of them.

We discussed it later and decided this anomaly could have been Bob Stafford, his ghostself. How unusual would that be? He died a tragic death, and his killers, although known, never received punishment from the law.

Stafford's murder occurred only five years after construction of his opera house. In the "ghost world," he could desire to visit from time to time to watch the audience enjoy shows he was initially responsible for over a 120 years ago. Who knows? Houdini may be accompanying him. And we know Houdini could escape into the light any time he wanted.

The Stafford Opera House
425 Spring Street
Columbus, Texas 78934
979-732-5135
www.columbustexas.org

Sugar Land

The sugar industry developed first, then the unique town of Sugar Land emerged. Samuel M. Williams received a land grant in 1828. His two brothers Nathaniel and Mathew joined him.

Mathew created Oakland Plantation, growing corn, sugarcane, and cotton. They formed a raw sugar mill in 1843. Ten years later, Benjamin Terry and William Kyle purchased the raw plantation. The former organized Terry's Texas Rangers during the Civil War and were responsible for naming the town. But after their deaths in 1861 and 1864, the plantation waned. E. H. Cunningham came to the rescue and invested a million dollars in a sugar refinery and a new raw-sugar mill.

Since the town was based around the sugar industry from the beginning, it's important to know that much labor came from the prison farms, located nearby. Many of the prisoners fell victim to fever epidemics, in part because of their work in wet sugarcane fields. And mosquitoes were partially responsible for their illnesses. The convicts called Sugar Land the "Hell hole on the Brazos," because of the brutal working conditions.

In the first decade of the twentieth century, Isaac Kempner and William Eldridge acquired the plantations and sugar company and formed the Sugar Land Industries and Sugar Land Railroad. The crops suffered from plant disease and saw their last harvest in 1928. From then on, Kempner and Eldridge imported raw sugar.

A steady development for the city began in 1959, and the population has grown to approximately 31,000 in 2009. The "sweet smell of success."

One Lump or Two?

The story is, in the old days, the Imperial Sugar Company in Sugar Land used a curious ingredient in the bleaching process: *bones*.

The company began its milling business in the mid-1880s. Sugarcane needed processing close to the cane fields because of its perishable nature.

Groans filtering down from the floor above in the sugar refinery did nothing to appease prisoners' fears of becoming sweetener for someone's cereal. You don't always have to see ghosts. Sometimes you hear them.

The prison system bought the 2,500-acre Harlem Farm on Oyster Creek. This land joined property of the Imperial Sugar Company during the period of 1928 through 1932. Imperial had built its refinery in 1925. They crushed the stalks, extracted juices, then condensed and boiled them into raw crystals. The coarse brown substance was then ready for refining. The state augmented Harlem's size by purchasing more adjacent lands for prisoners to farm the crops. Several privately owned plantations had already succeeded in using convict labor.

Subsequently, the company decided to use convicts to work in its refinery. Since they were right next door, the owner found it easy to obtain more workers. The prison farm and the refinery operated together to produce sugar. When Beauford Jester became governor of Texas, they changed the name to the Jester State Prison Farm.

John C. Allwright, historian, author, and former volunteer in the genealogy department of Brown Memorial Library in Richmond, made a study of area legends. He shared eerie information concerning the refinery.

The company contracted with suppliers to furnish bones on a regular basis. Consider the fact convicts often died in prison. If no one claimed a body, the warden ordered the remains buried on prison grounds.

In 1903, Texas law required the filing of official death records. If a doctor knew nothing of a person's demise, no one knew to file a record. An obituary may have appeared in an area newspaper but not necessarily in a courthouse. The Refinery personnel did not always file these records. If a convict died while working at the refinery, what really became of his remains if there was no family to notify?

One supplier of bones to the refinery hired a few unethical employees. According to Mr. Allwright, they mixed human bones with those of animals. When the bleaching process began, moaning echoed from the top floor.

After word circulated concerning the use of human bones, convicts demanded not to work at the refinery. They preferred staying in the prison, even in solitary confinement.

Since the foreman realized he had to do something about the eerie sounds, he ordered the bones and sugar moved. The moaning stopped in the refinery but continued at a rapid pace in the new storage area.

Workers still heard sounds and insisted objects moved. Not only that, they felt surrounded by something they couldn't see.

In 1913, guards at the farm confined convicts in what they referred to as the "dark cell." The enclosure, about nine- by seven-feet and less than seven-feet high, offered little or no air. The temperature soon rose to more than one hundred degrees. The men screamed for help, but guards did not respond.

By the time they opened the door, eight men were dead. Suffocated. An investigation found the prison officials used "bad judgment." They filed no other charges. No one knows for certain what became of the prisoners' remains.

The Imperial Sugar Company's refinery and distribution center closed in 2003, and the refinery now stands vacant. At this writing, plans for turning the structure into something benefiting the community have been set aside. The difficulty and expense of maintaining it wasn't practical. It does hold much historical value, and that's not all it holds. There may still be moaning coming from the old refinery today.

Sugar companies have used new methods of processing for years. So sit down and enjoy sugar in your tea or coffee—no bones about it.

The land which the old sugar factory occupied was sold for the development of residential neighborhoods, parks, businesses, and lakes, in keeping with the historic qualities of the town. Whatever spirits have lingered there for long over a century may choose to remain in Sugar Land. How sweet it is.

HOBO JOE

John Allwright had this information firsthand. His family knew a railroad detective who worked out of the Houston office. The story took place many decades ago, and unfortunately, I can't pinpoint the location—only a small bridge between Sugar Land and Richmond.

As a freight train approached a small bridge crossing over a creek, a man appeared on the tracks. The night was moonless, and the engineer, whom I shall refer to as Ken, could see only the distance covered by the engine's lights.

At the instant Ken spied the man standing on the tracks, he knew he couldn't stop in time. He applied the brakes immediately, saying a prayer along with that action. Sweat pouring from the engineer's forehead at what should have been the time of impact, the man on the tracks vanished.

The area was highly wooded, so Ken assumed the man had disappeared into the trees. He merely thought it was unusual, though frightful at the time. Soon, however, when he began talking about it, he learned this was not the first such occurrence. On a fairly regular basis, other engineers had made the same report. It happened only with freights, never with passenger trains.

The engineer drove his car to the bridge, thinking the man might be camped in the area. He called, hoping the man would come forth, but he didn't. On future runs, the image appeared just as before, and Ken would always apply the brakes.

Perhaps he was more inquisitive than other engineers, always having been interested in ghosts, so he checked railroad records in Fort Bend County. Finding nothing there, he inquired at the County Sheriff's Office. Nothing there, either.

At that point he decided to talk to a couple engineers who vowed they, too, had seen the vanishing man. One told him he was aware of a hobo who would get on the undercarriage of a freight car. Whatever his destination, he obviously returned on another car at a later date, and in a week or so, he'd ride out again on the undercarriage. They figured the hobo had decided to stay at the earlier destination point, because they never saw him again.

Dave sensed there was an answer if only he could find it. Stubborn, he obtained a handcar and traveled down to the bridge. Weeds stood tall both winter and summer. He hopped off the car and tramped through the high grasses. Startled, he half expected but partly hoped he was wrong, he almost stepped on human remains.

He returned to the railcar and headed back to town. After reporting his discovery to the Fort Bend County Sheriff's office, they ordered an inquest. They found no identification on the body, but one of the engineers told the sheriff the clothes were the same as worn by the hobo, and he knew his name to be Joe.

After his burial, Hobo Joe's ghost never appeared again to the engineers, nor to anyone else—at least that we know of.

Small bridge between Sugar Land and Richmond

RICHMOND

Richmond, the county seat of Fort Bend County, is fifteen miles southwest of Houston, on the Brazos River. Every town begins somewhere, and a log fort was the starting point at the bend of the river for Richmond, a historical town and one that always welcomes visitors.

It fairly well dissolved during the Runaway Scrape of 1836, but William Lusk and Robert Eden Handy brought it back to life when they sold lots to mark the town's new beginning. The Republic of Texas incorporated it in May 1837. Its early residents also included Erastmus (Deaf) Smith, after whom a county is named, and Mirabeau B. Lamar. A few years after the 1853 yellow fever epidemic, the railroad came through, and Richmond became a prosperous market and shipping center.

Even though the town's economy suffered during the Civil War, it remained isolated from the war itself. The close proximity of Rosenberg, as well as other new communities that cropped up in the area, created a rivalry. A massive flood struck in 1899. After recovery, its economy centered on agriculture, then oilfields and a sulphur mine. The prosperity brought people back to town, with many commuting to jobs in Houston.

The town developed, and as a result the population in 2009 grew to over 14,000, not including the many cats I noticed wandering the residential neighborhoods. And I definitely noticed Richmond's one-way streets and the presence of patrol cars (worth remembering).

With Richmond's historical background and friendly atmosphere, it's no wonder ghosts of times gone by also reside there. Each has its story to tell.

MOANS AN' GROANS AN' GALLOWS

If you stand dead center in Fort Bend County, you will be in its oldest community. Richmond, with a small town atmosphere, has big town features. Some call it quaint. All call it friendly. Even the ghosts in the Old Richmond Jail appear to be likeable sorts.

If a prisoner's ghost chooses to roam the jail, who can blame him? The jailer threw the prisoner's human form into a ready-made grave because no one claimed his remains.

In the founding of the community in 1822, Stephen F. Austin's colonists discovered a bend in the Brazos River when they sailed up the broad waterway. They chose the spot for protection and called it "Fort Bend." By 1824, because of the rich land and navigable river, the population increased and incorporated thirteen years later.

With so many settlers, a jail would be at the top of the "need" list. The town had previous jails that three clever little pigs could have dismantled. But then came a sturdy brick structure that has stood for more than a hundred years. At present, it houses the Richmond Police Department and one or more ghosts. A new jail stands just behind the old one. It offers lodging for law-breakers—no reservations needed and no room service available.

"Eerie footsteps and groans at night . . ." Something passes a doorway. The something has no identity other than a misty shape. The hall is empty, and passing cars do not cast the shadow.

There must be another explanation.

A friend of John Allwright's father served as a prison guard from 1905 to 1930. The guard told of the time he made a bed check and found a prisoner missing. The man had committed a dreadful crime and constantly caused trouble within the prison.

Once he escaped his cell, he found real freedom a problem. He had to forget west or south, because the Brazos River framed both sides. Since Oyster Creek ran on the east, the only logical route led him toward Houston. Exhausted, he needed to hide before daylight, because a search party of guards and dogs was hot on his trail. He climbed the first big tree that could give him shelter until nightfall. Thinking he found the right limb on which to rest, he grew a bit too comfortable and fell asleep. He somehow shifted positions and lost his footing.

As the dogs followed his scent, they became agitated. Growling, they tracked him to the tree, stopped and barked incessantly at finding their man. Seeing a hand in the leaves, a guard called for him to come down. Neither the man nor his hand moved. A guard fired a warning shot into the branches. This did not bring down the convict, so one of the men climbed the tree to get him. To his amazement, he found the man's neck caught in a fork of the tree. He had served as his own executioner.

The legend is, since the guards shot the convict full of holes after he was already dead, his ghost has haunted the prison for years. His apparition appears in daylight, as well as night.

Another tale concerns the county's museum and surrounding property. One director of the museum's archaeological department has taken groups of children on digs at the George Ranch and Old Richmond Jail. They looked for pieces of pottery or whatever artifacts they might find hidden beneath the soil.

Each of these locations had an abandoned well where people discarded items to make the dangerous holes safe. Such articles also lie in shallow soil around the area. The children would dig into the well and bring up their "treasures." They shoveled out buckets of dirt. They dug so deep, they heard moans—not the well's echo. The children scattered.

Allwright researched and discovered a prisoner had died in his cell many years ago. Since no one claimed the prisoner's remains, the jailer dropped his body into the well and shoveled dirt on top of him. If the museum director had not allowed children to dig there in the first place, we wouldn't have known about the "ghost in the well."

People speculate about the spooky incidents, and this speculation brings attention from the curious, as well as police and office workers. We have heard the phrase, "a friend of a friend said a friend said. . . ." In this case, people who worked in the building have either experienced something weird or know someone who has.

In 1955, someone purchased the building and sold most of the steel bars for scrap. In the late 1970s, the Fort Bend County Museum accepted the jail as a donation. The Confederate Museum leased it in the 1980s, after which it remained vacant until the city renovated it.

Richmond's police department then returned to its home in the remodeled jail. The colorful history remained, for people still report ghost sightings.

The police no longer use solitary confinement cells in the basement. Even so, some employees, whose offices are on the floor above, have reported hearing eerie footsteps and groans at night. These are not sounds of creaking floorboards.

A few officers who type reports from their desks say they have seen something pass by the doorway. An employee observed a shadow in a mirror when no one else was in the room. Rial was certain someone had entered, then realized she was alone—as far as mortals go.

A paranormalist, who spent a night there, reported seeing an unidentifiable shape in one of the cells by the gallows. The gallows used in the late 1800s combine with a stairway. Because of possible structural damage if removed, they continue to be an eerie reminder of the past. Records show only two men have been hanged there. A lynching did take place outside, and perhaps more we don't know about. Not every lynching found its way into a ledger.

At one time, Sgt. Steve Eiteman provided tours of the old building. Although he never heard any strange noises, he heard reports of such. Eiteman explained his theories on who the ghost and/or ghosts might be.

In 1898, Pete Autrey and Emanuel Morris hanged for killing Fannie Williams. Morris maintained his innocence. In an article from the "*Rockdale Messenger*, dated Thursday, 3 Nov 1898: 'Two murderers Hung – Richmond, Texas, Oct. 30 – Pete Autrey and Emanuel Morris, convicted of separate crimes dropped through the gallows at the county jail on Friday afternoon.'" It would appear they had separate trials for the same crime.

If Morris's claim of innocence were true, he would be a likely suspect for a ghost. An apparition appeared soon after the hanging. If the ghost who makes these visits really is Morris, could he be searching for records to clear himself?

According to Cheryl Skinner, columnist for *the Fort Bend Star*, the former Police Captain George Paruch, said he received complaints from the cleaning lady as well as the night dispatcher. They each had heard "some things that were just eerie and spooky." Although the captain had not heard these sounds, the police contacted Father Howard Drawback of the Sacred Heart Catholic Church. He blessed the building in 1999, soon after the police department moved back into it.

The department maintains a small museum of photographs, badges, guns, and other memorabilia. They use old cells on the second floor for storage and interrogation.

Now if someone could only interrogate a ghost.

Old Richmond Jail
(Now the Police Department)
600 Preston Street
Richmond, Texas 77469

Birds of a Different. . .

The door had not opened. Where did he come from? The museum director heard nothing.

Still, the unmistakable figure of a man stood by the desk of Lana Dunkerly, communications director of the Fort Bend Museum Complex.

The man soon began pointing out where certain doors and corridors used to be—decades earlier—long before the museum's remodeling. He knew "way too much" about the house's history. Dunkerly thought he looked familiar. Then she recalled she first noticed him riding a bicycle on Richmond's streets. On one occasion, Dunkerly heard a shutter slamming. The wind couldn't have blown it—not on a still day. When she investigated, the room was empty. During board meetings, members left to see what caused the weird sounds drifting down from the floor above. They did not find an answer.

Pete Shifflet, a tour guide, had seen the stranger in the hardware store. The man commented he had ridden by the store and saw a woman dressed in "Texas clothing" of years long past. In the old days, hardware stores sold piece goods. So far, the apparition isn't identified.

The Museum Complex offers a hundred years of the area's history. But the main subject of this tale is the McFarlane House and its revenant residents—all part of the Complex. Isaac McFarlane, a native of Scotland, served with Terry's Texas Rangers during the Civil War. He lived in Richmond in an impressive home. McFarlane House played an important part in the historical Jaybird—Woodpecker War of the 1880s. This feud between two political factions, each seeking control of Fort Bend County, led to several deaths.

Even though the Republicans emerged winners in the election of 1888, assaults, threats, and two more deaths occurred. In August 1889, the inevitable transpired, and the county became an armed camp. Gunfire left heavy casualties around the courthouse, hotel, and on the second floor of McFarlane House.

The first museum underwent a renovation a hundred years later, so they moved their displays into the McFarlane House for that year. John Allwright, overseer of the project, opened the house at ten in the mornings and closed at four. He had been there three weeks when something strange occurred. He heard the front door open and close but didn't see anyone enter. The same morning, footsteps sounded from the second floor, but Allwright investigated and found no explanation.

Arthur Schultz once rented the house for an appliance and TV business. After twenty years he moved out, and Mr. McFarlane's grandson, Clarence, donated the house to the city.

Allwright said Mr. and Mrs. Schultz once stopped by to see how the remodeling was going. When Allwright told him of hearing footsteps, Schultz related his own experience. He and his wife had also heard them. Hoping to establish proof, he spread flour beneath all the windows and at both doors. The house also had a trapdoor, by which he sprinkled flour. He found no prints the following morning, but still heard someone walking up the stairs.

He searched the house but never found a visitor. "Footsteps are still heard there today," Allwright said.

McFarlane now contains the administrative offices of the Museum Association. According to a *Fort Bend Star* article by David Rosen, the staff has reported unnatural occurrences.

Several of both factions died during this bitter feud in the 1880s. But is the ghost a Jaybird or a Woodpecker? If only someone were to find a feather . . . .

The McFarlane House
500 Houston Street
Richmond, Texas 77469
For Information: 281-342-6478

The McFarlane House.

THE JANE LONG-SMITH COTTAGE

Built in the late 1830s, the Long-Smith Cottage was first owned by Jane Long, the "Mother of Texas," and later owned by Goliad survivor Thomas Jefferson Smith (thus named Long-Smith Cottage). It has been on museum property since 1987. One of the oldest buildings in Richmond, its furnishings show class life in Richmond during the 1840s and 1860s. The hand-made furniture includes articles once belonging to Jane Long. Jane Long once owned most of the land on which the town of Richmond now sits.

The Jane Long-Smith Cottage is located next to the Fort Bend Museum in Richmond.

Jane Long, born in 1798, was the tenth child of Captain William Mackall Wilkinson and his wife, Anne Dent. When Jane's father died a year later, the family moved to Mississippi Territory. After her mother's

Jane Long's house hasn't changed much.

death, she lived with a sister in Natchez. During this time, she met and married James Long.

Eventually, after the Spanish troops from San Antonio headed for the frontier outpost, she fled with other American families. James Long arranged for Jane to go to Bolivar Peninsula on Galveston Bay. Several families lived at Fort Las Casas when Long left for La Bahia in 1821. Jane expected James back within a month. When he hadn't returned, she learned he was captured and taken to Mexico City. He was accidentally killed seven months later.

Jane had lost one daughter and was pregnant with her third child. Having virtually no money or food, she traveled with her two little daughters to San Antonio to apply for a pension. Months later, having collected nothing, she left. Eventually, after several moves and the death of her youngest daughter, she arrived in Richmond at the age of thirty-nine. She had received a land title in Fort Bend County, where she managed to open a boarding house, then raised cattle and cotton with the help of twelve slaves.

After she became a widow, leading men of Texas courted her: Ben Milam, Mirabeau Lamar, Sam Houston. Lamar planned to write the history of Texas and asked her to tell her life experiences. We know her history primarily from what she had told Mirabeau Lamar in 1837.

When her married daughter died in 1870, Jane could no longer manage her diminished estate. She died at the home of her grandson and was buried in the Morton Cemetery in Richmond.

Jane's cottage is open for scheduled tours. Spirits have no need for official touring. They know all there is to know, especially if one happens to be Jane herself. The front gate, as well as the house, is always locked. The quaint little frame house is surrounded by a white-picket fence. A tour guide explains the furnishings that visitors can see from the doorway. The bed has a straw mattress, much the same as Jane Long would have had when she lived there.

The structure is not without its spirit. One strange occurrence takes place, not daily, but often. It is as if someone has sat on the edge of the bed, then got up, leaving an indentation.

Neatly making up the bed and reversing the mattress makes no difference. Or, perhaps the ghost doesn't get up at all, and we just can't see. The guide, however, raises the iron bar at the doorway and straightens the bed. In no time at all, it appears someone has again sat on it. Now if the house and windows are locked at night, who gets in to sit on the bed?

According to an article by Marquita Griffin in the October 30, 2007 issue of the *Fort Bend Herald*, Cathy Tagliabue told her that a stain appeared around the indentation on the quilt. As time passed, the stain grew darker until the staff replaced the quilt. The indentations didn't cease, but the stain did not return. Even many of the most skeptical believe Jane Long's spirit lives in her house. With such an emotional and traumatic life, it makes sense she would want to find peace in her home in Richmond.

Jane Long-Smith Cottage
500 Houston Street
Richmond, Texas 77469
281-342-6478

THE HAUNTING OF MOORE HOUSE

Included in the Fort Bend Museum Complex is the John M. Moore Home, a neoclassical structure built in 1883. The two-story mansion has six massive columns at the entry, extending from the ground floor to the roofline. You can take yourself back in time by walking from the front entry gate to the mansion steps—as if invited to a Christmas gala 125 years ago.

Mr. Moore built his house large enough to accommodate guests, who often enjoyed their visit so much, they stayed several days. They occasionally stayed longer if they traveled by buggy from far away. Imagine standing on the second-floor balcony, which covers the enormous width of the house, watching the next carriage drive up and wondering who the guests would be.

In those years, people who had the money hired a teacher for their children. Often in wealthier families, a separate cottage close to the main house served as a school, even with lodging for the teacher. John and his wife, Lottie Dyer, designed an upstairs room as a schoolroom. The tutor didn't live in the house but came on a regular basis to teach the children.

Mr. Moore included a fruit cellar on his property, but in case of a storm, the cellar served as protection. Mr. Allwright related to me that ladies from the church also held quilting bees upstairs. Moore was obviously a generous man. Because they had several children, he and his wife designated one room as a birthing room.

One of their daughters returned home when the time came for her baby to be born. A chair sat in the room for the new mother to rock her infant. Unfortunately, the daughter died in childbirth and her baby later passed away. The chair began rocking.

The Moores' housekeeper for fifty years determined it was the ghost of the Moores' daughter who sat in the chair. Interestingly, the chair remained still whenever anyone else came into the room, but when the housekeeper entered, it moved. Since the two women shared a close friendship, the housekeeper thought the daughter felt comfortable whenever she entered. She truly believed the mother's ghost was rocking her baby.

Mr. Moore was a Texas congressman in 1905 to 1913. He was mayor of Richmond, a successful cattle rancher and also served as president of the Sons of the Republic of Texas.

In an article, "The Moore House," in the *Fort Bend Herald*, October 30, 2007, Marquita Griffin interviewed Rick Taylor, special project coordinator for the museum. Taylor remarked on a particular incident

The Magnificent Moore House.

from a few years previous. A tour guide escorted a small group through the house when a little girl wanted to know, "Why is that man sitting in the chair over there?"

This was not the rocking chair. Taylor said that no one should have been sitting in the chair. And the guide ended the tour. He must have felt a strong presence of an ethereal being to have stopped when he did.

The Texas Paranormal Researchers came in to check if a ghost or ghosts were indeed there. While they did not observe anything unusual, the ghost meter dropped considerably in temperature at one specific spot, denoting a spirit was present.

Perhaps it is Mr. Moore. Or, as the housekeeper said, "The Moores' daughter and her baby." Nobody's talking.

The Moore House
406 South 5th Street
Richmond, Texas 77469
For Information: 281-342-6478

AND TELL OF TIME

It all started with a clock. A sundial would've been less trouble. And with a sundial, there would have been no ghost in the Fort Bend County Courthouse.

The city has a rich history. It was the site of one of the original colonies in Texas and formed from a land grant from Stephen F. Austin. The settlement of the county started in the early 1820s, under the Anglo-American colonization of Texas. In 1822, a small group of men from Austin's following traveled inland less than a hundred miles and settled on a bluff near a deep bend in the river. They decided on Fort Bend as the name. The more colonists who came in, the Karankawa Indians began moving out.

The first courthouse built in 1842 cost $600. Actually, it *was* a house. This changed eight years later when John Herndon built a two-story brick building, costing $6,000. Over twenty years passed before the third one, and the fourth came in 1883. The 1900 hurricane severely damaged it. The county judge at the time, as well as the commissioners, thought the courthouse was too small. Besides, with so many necessary repairs, they decided to build a new one.

Enter C. H. Page and Brothers, eminent architects, especially of courthouses. The judge had specific ideas as to the dome and clock face locations. The Pages had just completed the Hays County Courthouse the previous year. The buildings were almost identical. The judge, however, was adamant about the way the dome would look from all sides of the courthouse. The architects struggled to figure out the proper balance. They built three versions in various counties before they mastered it on the Anderson Courthouse in 1914.

The judge wanted four faces on the clock, so people could see the time from all directions.

This was not uncommon later on, but somewhat rare in early nineteenth-century Texas. He wanted the clock to strike not only every hour but every half-hour as well. When considering there were less than 1,200 people in the town, they would all hear the clock—a lot.

The clock needed winding every eight days. The judge engaged a man to take care of it, and everything went smoothly for about four years, until the clock broke. That's one clock, four faces. The man who had been winding it didn't know how to do repairs, so the judge contacted someone in Houston. Now Richmond is only a few miles west of Houston, and he had to travel by train. Mr. Allwright, who told me this story, commented that the only other route was via a dirt trail.

But what time is it . . . really?

Everyone was glad to see him arrive one Friday mid-afternoon. Glad to be of help, although probably not that happy to devote an afternoon away from Houston, he took his tools and climbed the steep ladder to the tower. The people downstairs heard the chink-chink sounds and an occasional hammer and felt the man was well on his way to completing the repairs. The clock would chime once again.

The employees were ready to leave for the weekend, and assuming the man would be finished soon, he could find his own way out.

The unthinkable occurred. When he had not returned to work in Houston on Monday morning, the company called the county judge. The employees told the judge they left by 5:00 on Friday. The judge felt something terrible was wrong and rushed to climb the ladder, hoping his suspicions were not true.

When he got to the tower, he was horrified to see the man lying dead. It was apparently a heart attack, but even if he had called out, there was no one downstairs to hear him.

The man had finished the repairs before he died. But an unusual thing happened later. The clock would be working accurately, then strike 6:00 when it was only 1:00. Nobody came up with a plausible reason for those particular hours to strike.

Another repairman checked it out, and it worked properly, leaving everyone satisfied. But it again started striking at 6 and 1. Everybody came to the same conclusion. The repairman's ghost was still in the tower, toying with the clock.

But in the 1920s, they installed an electric mechanism, and from then on, all four faces kept correct time. That was the assumption . . . no one could ever see all faces at once.

Fort Bend County Courthouse
301 Jackson Street
Richmond, Texas 77469

A Swirling Vortex of Fear

We all know some rivers run wild. Think of the Rio Grande, the Mississippi, and Colorado—now there's a river for you. In the spring when snow melts, it swells into churning and dangerous water. But the Brazos is something else. At 1,260 miles, it's the longest in the state, flowing from New Mexico to Texas and passing through Richmond to the Gulf. It can be more than ten miles wide in some places, then narrow to a meandering stream. Peaceful may not always be what it seems.

Three Richmond teenaged girls had done their chores, sewed a little, then grew restless and bored. School would soon start for the fall session, and they wanted at least one exciting thing to talk about with their friends. So they began making plans for the next day.

The teenagers decided to build a raft and float down the Brazos to what people called Rocky Falls. It wasn't big as falls go, but water did fall over the rocks. Did they know how to build a raft? They thought so. The father of one of them had a stack of long logs, yet uncut for firewood, out by the barn. At fifteen, the oldest of the three retrieved a saw from the shed. The girls tried to even the ends at 8-foot lengths. They figured the approximate 8' x 8' raft would carry the three of them.

After positioning the logs next to one another, they took a coil of rope from the shed and threaded it over and under in three places, tying it securely. They then nailed four narrow strips of wood across to help keep them together. Perfect, providing the raft would stay afloat.

All who lived in the area knew that at one specific place in the riverbed, a row of large flat rocks spread from one side of the river to the other, forming a low-water bridge. No one knew who had placed them there, as the rocks weren't the kind found near Richmond. It couldn't have been a natural formation, so the theory was Indians had carried them there sometime in the century before.

The girls planned to make sandwiches and float the raft down to the falls, pull into the bank at some shady spot and have a picnic. They would swim and play where the water was usually clearer. Each one picked up a limb to guide the raft. Huckleberry Finn had nothing on them. It wasn't very deep through the section where the raft would be floating, and besides, the water from a past rain had settled days before.

What the girls didn't know was, because of recent heavy rains near Hempstead, to the north, the river had been rising. They guided the raft upstream where the water was fuller, thinking the momentum would carry them downstream without effort from them. But when they made a turn at the bend, an oncoming rush of water raced toward them. The surge hurled the raft downstream toward Rocky Falls, where it smashed into the rocks, pitching the girls into the swollen river.

Panicking, they began swimming to safety, when one of them went under. One of the girls tried to save her, but the swirling vortex was too swift. She had no choice but to swim back. Both of them reached the bank and turned to see their friend go under. She bobbed up once and went down again. But before their disbelieving eyes, the hazy figure of an Indian emerged from the water and carried her safely to the bank. He then vanished into a mist. An incredible story for the first day of school.

According to legend, the river received its name when Francisco Vazquez de Coronado and his men were about to die from thirst. Indians came out from the forest and led them to fresh water in a clear portion of the river. Gratefully, Coronado named it, *Los Brazos de Dios*, "The arms of God."

There are those who think Indian spirits still roam up and down the Brazos River. After all, the Karankawas were in the area long before the white man. The land is still theirs in spirit, and one spirit saved a young girl.

Rocky Falls
I don't know an address for Rocky Falls, except
that it's a spot in the Brazos River near Richmond.
Perhaps *you* have been there.

CLIPS

One might think a barbershop is a pleasant respite from a man's busy day—a place he can go to relax, have a haircut, and hear the latest happenings in a small town like Richmond. The Richmond Barber Shop is all that and more: "The best little clip joint west of the Brazos."

The business opened in 1913, a year after construction of the building. It is a small shop but adequate. Homer Sharp occupied the rear living quarters.

According to John Allwright, during an extreme winter, Mr. Sharp heard a rapping at the back door. Since Sharp had a skittish nature, he thought if he didn't open it, whoever it was would leave. The tragedy of his not answering the door? The next morning a cowboy lay frozen to death behind the home of Jane Long. But she apparently didn't open the door either, if indeed she heard the sound.

Since Mr. Sharp recognized the dead man as a customer of some years before, he figured that was the reason for his rapping on the door. He needed help from a friend. Sharp heard the knocking every winter since then in freezing weather. Sometimes he answered and sometimes not. He never saw a ghost, but as long as he lived there, the knocks continued.

The tales didn't stop, however, with Mr. Sharp's passing in 1985. A lot of hair has been swept from beneath the barber chairs since then, as well as the telling of many stories.

There will always be the superstitious and the skeptics. On one occasion, a customer entered for a haircut and beard trim. He quoted Biblical stories. Before he left, he pulled out a small piece of metal with engraving on it. It was written in Yiddish, and he didn't translate it, other than to say it was from Biblical times.

For some reason, which he didn't divulge, he stuck it above the barbershop door in a slight indentation so it would be secure. He warned whoever removed it would die on the spot. Since no one wanted to test the customer's prophecy, it remained. Besides, it was high up. Mr. Allwright vouched for how long it had stayed there. The weird thing is, the man never returned.

There have been different owners of the Richmond Barber Shop during the years. Many people have gone for haircuts since childhood. Some are over eighty years old. A gentleman bought the shop in 1972 from Mr. McFarland, a well-known citizen of Richmond.

One afternoon, the new owner went into the back room. His gaze fell to a small stool on which lay a metal object about 3" x 3" (having nothing to do with the piece of metal wedged above the door, as far as anyone

A little shop of ghosts?

knew). When he turned it over he realized it was a 1937 calendar, never used—all the months intact. Sand coated it, but no sand appeared on the stool or on the windowsills. No one has found an answer for the eerie discovery of such a calendar. Another paranormal aspect of the story is when the owner placed the stool out of the way when he closed for the night, it stood in its original place the following morning. No matter how often he shifted it, the stool moved.

The backdoor always stayed locked at night. One theory is, a ghost used the stool to reach the metal above the door, but it was untouched. The metal calendar is still a mystery.

Unfortunately, the day I was there the shop was closed. Should have known—it was Monday. So I didn't get to see for myself the place above the door.

Is this a little shop of ghosts? Customers know it as neat and inviting. The floor is always swept clean. Hair today . . . gone . . . no, I won't say it.

Richmond Barber Shop
315 Morton Street
Richmond, Texas 77469
281-232-2387

WEST COLUMBIA

The founders of the Republic of Texas chose West Columbia as the first state capitol. It remained so for only a few months, but there is no question, it and the surrounding area is the birthplace of Texas. The entire vicinity is surrounded by history. In town there is a replica of the First Capitol of the Republic of Texas. The stately Varner-Hogg Mansion also still stands, suffering minimal damage during the Hurricane Ike.

The town, located about forty miles southwest of Houston, has a population of approximately 5,000.

THE HOUNDS OF OROZIMBO

The original tale came from author Catherine Munson Foster of Brazoria County. She owned the land. Her 1977 book, *Ghosts Along the Brazos*, is out of print, but the story is there for the telling, ever since the Battle of San Jacinto.

The Orozimbo Plantation (named after an Indian chief), which Dr. James Aeneas E. Phelps owned in 1824, is gone now, destroyed by a hurricane in late 1936. In one of the last photographs taken, it showed a spacious two-story house with a large porch on the first and second stories. Tall oak trees in one of the oldest settlements in Texas surrounded the residence, with one enormous oak shading it. A picket fence ran across the front lawn, with horizontal log railings circling the house and outbuildings.

Orozimbo served a historic purpose. After Texas gained its independence, Sam Houston and his men captured the Mexican general, Santa Anna, when he tried to escape disguised in a soldier's standard uniform.

Houston had to safeguard him from revengeful families of his battle victims. He knew if he left Santa Anna unguarded, even for a moment, he would be a perfect target for murder.

Houston moved Santa Anna from one location to another. He knew as long as they held the general hostage, invasions of Texas would cease.

Dr. Phelps was a hospital surgeon in the army at San Jacinto and a friend of Houston's, so his plantation seemed to be the ideal locale for detaining the Mexican general—keeping his enemies at bay. The time period here was five years after the Battle of San Jacinto, after Goliad and the Alamo. Dr. Phelps and his wife, Rosetta, treated the general as a guest, although restricting him to certain quarters.

He was still a prisoner and tried to commit suicide by taking laudanum, rather than suffer the humility of his capture. When Dr. Phelps realized what the general had done, he "retrieved" his life and watched him more closely afterward. As time went on, Santa Anna apparently enjoyed himself, since he gave no more thought to suicide.

Even though Santa Anna remained at Orozimbo from July until November 1836, the thought of his being rescued never left the minds of his men. On a late evening as the sky darkened, one of his officers gathered several riders and extra horses. They remained a safe distance from the house until the officer managed to enter, pretending to be one of the general's imprisoned staff.

Dr. Phelps provided Santa Anna with wine and other amenities, like a gracious host would. The extra "prisoner" drugged the wine and offered it to the guards, who gladly accepted.

In a short time, they passed out.

Everyone else in the house had retired for the night. All Santa Anna had to do then was wait for rescue. He waited . . . and continued to wait. As the would-be rescuers were ready to break into the house, a sudden and terrifying sound of baying hounds tore through the silence.

When all the lamps came on, one after another, the soldiers fled. Dr. Phelps and his household, hearing the horses as they sped off, grabbed their weapons and rushed outside. Nothing but swirling dust remained in the glow of moonlight. For the rest of the night, and nights thereafter, Phelps increased the guard about the house.

But the hounds . . . where did they go? Everyone in the house had heard them. To whom did they belong? Not to Dr. Phelps. While they sounded like a huge pack, a servant declared only three. Two were shaggy. One, hairless. He remarked that their eyes seemed glazed, almost as if blind. The hounds did not return the following day, or the next, but their near frightening appearance kept the servants alert.

Soon after this incident, General Houston, then president of Texas, felt it would serve peace to free Santa Anna. In November 1836, the

Mexican general and his escort set out in a stagecoach for Washington. President Andrew Jackson liberated him, sending him home aboard a naval vessel.

In 1843, during the Mier Expedition, one of the captured Texans did not go undetected.

Santa Anna recognized a name on the list, that of Orlando Phelps and knew he was Dr. Phelps's son. The general saved Orlando from execution and released him from prison in Salado. He gave him $500 in gold, new clothes, and a letter of credit with safe passage to Texas.

History tells us that for years the Mexican general sent presents to the Phelps family at Christmas, in return for the good treatment he received while at Orozimbo.

When Orlando Phelps returned home, he learned more about the hounds. A traveler came by and volunteered he had seen them. He even identified them as having belonged to a neighbor.

The dogs never disobeyed their master and loved him as he did them. They were always close to his side. When the day came their master left to fight in the War for Independence, he instructed his hounds to stay behind. They obeyed but soon grew restless, and after a while, stopped eating. They eventually disappeared—surely to search for their master, his last command lost in their loneliness.

People for miles around heard of the hounds. Citizens of West Columbia had seen them from time to time. They would crouch in the shadows, eyes glowing from within dense palmetto thickets. Two unkempt and tangled, the other, thin and void of hair.

If walking by the deep coastal forests along the Brazos River, where Spanish moss hangs from trees like long beards, a man could think someone or some thing lurked nearby. When he would turn, only glazed eyes watched.

Dr. Phelps died in 1847. His burial site is on the property near the plantation house. In 1981 campers set a fire, and the famous and majestic Orozimbo oak tree burned. All that is left now is a stone monument dedicated to Dr. Phelps and his cotton plantation.

SITE OF "OROZIMBO"
"HOME OF DR. JAMES A. E. PHELPS,
A MEMBER OF 'OLD THREE HUNDRED' OF
AUSTIN'S COLONY, HOSPITAL SURGEON
OF THE TEXAS ARMY AT SAN JACINTO.
HERE SANTA ANNA WAS DETAINED AS A
PRISONER FROM JULY TO NOVEMBER, 1836"

As far as I know, the phantom dogs remain unfound. Someone reported seeing them in 1974 near Phelps's gravesite and what remains of the big oak. Some believe they still look for their master who never returned. They are unaware he died at Goliad and continue their search. According to old-timers in Brazoria County, they've roamed the dense woodlands for decades. Is it possible? Over 185 years?

You won't see them during the day. You might not see them at all. But some evening when clouds have covered the moon, drive down the back roads and stop every now and then. Listen closely. You might hear the howling of the Hounds of Orozimbo.

The Orozimbo Plantation
The site of the plantation is a few miles from West Columbia (north on CR 25, then 1.0 mile east on CR 255 to the locked gate). The stone historical monument is about 100 yards inside the gate, on private property.

Bailey's Prairie

The village of Bailey's Prairie was named after James Britton Bailey, a North Carolinian and veteran of the War of 1812. Bailey located in the area first, and the town grew up around him. Sugar plantations and cattle ranching were the main operations. The population in 1972 was 228 and grew to 694 in the 2000 census.

During the day at Bailey's Prairie, the sun obliterated any ball of light shining through the trees, or even from the clearing. I fully expected to see that light, but I was there in the morning. It must be an after dark thing. Many stories concern this fella named Brit Bailey, and they don't all agree. Brit didn't agree on much of anything, either.

If you're in the right place at the right time in Bailey's Prairie, you might get a chill or two—not from winter's cold, but from an eerie ball of light. Some say the light belongs to Brit Bailey.

Whiskey, Well-Aged

Now just about everybody has heard of, or read about Brit, at least those interested in Texas history and eerie tales of the paranormal world. His full name was James Briton Bailey, born in North Carolina in 1779. Brit married early, and he and his wife, Edith Smith, had six children. After her death, he married her sister, Nancy—a frequent pattern, marrying sisters in those days, and besides, they were often handy. A discrepancy in genealogical research suggests he had three wives, including one named Dorothy. Other records indicate Nancy and Dorothy were the same person.

The Baileys had moved to Kentucky, where he served in the legislature; however, he didn't have the best reputation. Nothing serious—just a little forgery and a stint in a Kentucky prison, but that gives a foreshadowing of his character. He decided it was a good idea to leave the state and chose Tennessee, where he served as a captain in the U.S. Navy.

About 1818, Bailey packed up his family, and they brought their six slaves to Texas where he occupied land granted him by the Spanish government. Even though Stephen F. Austin knew of Bailey's previous reputation and questioned his land purchase, he eventually let him keep the land and remain in the Old Three Hundred. He also allowed Bailey to take an oath of fidelity to the Constitution of 1824, at which time Bailey became a lieutenant.

Even though he gained a name for himself by surviving various military battles, he also became known for his eccentricities and his penchant for brawling. He apparently enjoyed a good fight—or even a bad fight. Now and then he would just sit on the front porch and think of something to argue about.

Records show Bailey died of cholera December 6, 1832. Some thought the cause was orneriness. A modern-day autopsy, however, might find liver disease the real cause. A suitable epitaph could be, "Brit Bailey, lover of the whiskey jug."

Used to having his way, Bailey made sure his will specified his desire to be buried "facing west" in a standing position, so he could continue walking in the life beyond. He declared he had not only moved westward all his life, but he never looked up to any man. He didn't want it said, "Here lies old Brit Bailey, but rather, "Here stands Brit Bailey." He also wanted his rifle by his side and a whiskey jug at his feet—a jug filled with whiskey.

He believed his wife would carry out his wishes, but she had other ideas. Yes, she would see he had his rifle for the afterlife, but the whiskey jug? Not quite. She threw it away, saying it was high time he remained sober. The jug did not accompany Brit to the great barroom in the sky. He would probably have drunk its contents on the way.

After Brit's death and at the reading of his will, two of his daughters by the first Mrs. Bailey, claimed Nancy wasn't his legal wife. Eventually, the court favored their plea.

Now you know the man. I'll introduce you to his ghost. As early as 1850, reports of a weird light hovering in Bailey's Prairie attracted everyone's attention. It was vertical, moving, sometimes in circles. From those who professed to have seen it, it almost has a human form.

Brit and his family lived in a cabin, but after he became successful with cotton, cattle, and land, he had a house built—a red house. His burial site was just behind it under the shade of a giant oak tree, referred to later as Bailey's Oak. For years after, residents of the house vowed his ghost had visited them during the night.

Uncle Bubba, Bailey's manservant, claimed he saw apparitions in the house and an occasional fireball, which rose from Bailey's grave, then floated across the prairie. The over 100-year-old gentleman, with a fringe of white hair, remembered well. He vowed he promised Bailey he would place the whiskey jug in his coffin, but Mrs. Bailey grabbed it from him. Later on, John Thomas purchased the house and land. He didn't put much stock in the rumors the house was haunted—didn't believe in ghosts and such. So when he left his wife while gone on a trip, he returned to hear how she was frantic from seeing a ghost in the bedroom where she slept—the room where Brit died. Mr. Thomas teased her a little and said he'd sleep in the room that night. It wasn't much later when Mrs. Thomas heard her husband scream out. He swore he had seen the ghost of Ol' Brit Bailey.

Not long after that incident, the Thomases moved from the red house and didn't look back.

It remained empty for some time and eventually began to deteriorate. Something was different on Bailey's Prairie. Neighbors knew Brit was gone, but yet he was still there.

From time to time, people reported seeing a light moving through the trees. It moved slowly until someone tried to see what it was. The light would then speed beyond anyone's catching up with it. Animals acted strangely. They chose not to chase it, but rather cowered, as dogs and horses are innately sensitive to ghosts. As time went on, the light grew smaller. The word spread that the light was Brit Bailey, still looking for his whiskey jug. He had always had his way and was determined to have it once more, even in death.

The light eventually took the shape of a single ball, floating four to six feet above ground. It is safe to say that in the early nineteenth century, Texans knew nothing of electromagnetic energy, as in orb. Follow the ball's movements and it looks as if it is searching, searching. No need to ask for what. Could Bailey's light actually be Bailey's ghost? Or is that how rumors get started?

Nevertheless, a light is there, unexplained to skeptics, as well as to believers.

With the advent of the automobile, cars reportedly stopped, as if the key fell from the ignition. The same kind of thing happens with cameras, recorders, or other battery-operated equipment when a specter is near.

According to Catherine Munson Foster, whose family many years ago purchased the land called Bailey's Prairie, the light appears during the fall—long after dark. She also wrote that the light's appearances have decreased in the last decades, possibly making an appearance every seven years. If my calculations are correct, that would make it . . . uhm, I just missed it. . . .

The light has been known to chase vehicles on the highway late at night or very early in the morning. If frequency of reports have slacked at all, perhaps Ol' Brit's drinking habits are waning. He's been on the wagon a long time, so it wouldn't exactly be cold turkey.

The village of Bailey's Prairie reports no one has ever really proved what causes the ball of light to appear over the area. For lack of any better solution, the consensus is Ol' Brit is still frustrated, lookin', lookin'. . .

Bailey's Prairie
The town is on HW 35, between Angleton and West Columbia. Follow Farm Road 521 about 1.4 miles south from its intersection with HW 35. A marker is on HW 35 (roadside park) west of Angleton.

Arcadia Evergreen Cemetery

First came Arcadia, then came Santa Fe in Galveston County. Well, that isn't exactly true. The Coco Indians were there first and probably had their own name for it.

Henry Runge laid out the town in 1890 and called it Hall's Station. Arcadia soon became the name, and it was its own busy little town. In 1830, Asa Brigham founded its close neighbor, Alta Loma, with a grant from the Mexican government. The two communities remained as they were until Santa Fe annexed them both almost a century after Runge founded Hall's Station.

Just past 1900, my great-aunt Lizzie Hawkins Romine lived in Alta Loma when the school had eighty-nine pupils and only two teachers. Four of those pupils belonged to my great-aunt and uncle. Uncle Henry was in the dairy business, which was the area's largest industry, along with fruit and beef cattle. Arcadia's population had grown to 275 by 1947 and by 1980, it was within Santa Fe's boundaries.

Santa Fe, the name coming from the railroad, was originally considered coastal prairie, with lands suitable for grazing and rice production. Truck farming gained in popularity as forms of income. It's only twenty minutes from Houston and close enough to Galveston that boating and beaches are available. Arcadia and Alta Loma are no more, except in history books and old maps.

"Thank You, Thank You"

Arcadia Evergreen Cemetery, next to Dickinson Bayou, in Santa Fe, is more eerie at night than any cemetery I have visited. This particular story came to light because both my grandfather and great-grandfather are buried there. The latter, Andrew J. Hawkins and my great-grandmother, Permelia Nickell Hawkins, migrated from Kentucky to George's Creek, Somervell County, Texas, in 1880. They lived there until Permelia's death in 1899. This tale has a back story.

After the lil ol' boll weevil crossed the southern border and found its way to North Texas, cotton was no longer "king." The siblings dispersed from their homes, with one daughter, Lizzie Frances, moving to the Alta Loma and Arcadia area in Galveston County. After Permelia's death, Great-grandfather Andrew made his home with Lizzie, her husband, Henry, and their family.

Andrew died during a vicious Galveston hurricane in 1909. The storm washed out 200 feet of bridge leading to town. There was no one available to embalm Andrew, so they couldn't transport him to George's Creek for burial next to Permelia. A friend, Jim Adams Locke, took a detour to town and returned with a casket and new suit of clothes for Andrew's services in Arcadia's Evergreen Cemetery.

After my grandmother Anna Shults, Lizzie's sister, died young in 1903, my grandfather, Jim Shults, also moved to Arcadia with his two little children. He became a Deputy Sheriff for the county. In 1911, while changing cars, a prisoner pushed him off a train. The train caught him under its wheels, killing him instantly. Jim Shults was also interred in Evergreen.

Tragedy didn't stop there. The same year, Lizzie took ill. Doctors diagnosed her ailment as appendicitis. During surgery, the physician realized Lizzie had terminal cancer. Since she knew she would soon die, she dictated a "Letter Edged in Black," which is among 200 of my great-grandmother Permelia's family letters. When the letter arrived, its envelope with a black rim, the family knew it contained tragic news. Following are excerpts from her 1911 letter:

"... Bury me in white by the side of my dear little girl Junnie. And keep our graves clean and nice, with flowers on all four of them. Put tombs on them as soon as you can.

"I want the songs in Gospel Gleaners sung, Numbers 209, 139, 113, 40, 208. If they can't sing these, others will do.

"Children, all be good to each other. Do all you can, each of you do your part to get along nicely. Be good to ma and papa, and papa good to you.

"Treat everyone nice and good, especially old people so you will have lots of good friends.

"Let my sisters and brother know of my death at once. Just give all some little keepsake.

"Don't buy an expensive coffin or clothes for me.

"Save all you can to take care of these precious children.

Your wife and Mother,
Lizzie Romine"

Desecration of the Evergreen Cemetery began at least as early as 1950. Head stones of Jim Shults and Andrew Hawkins are among those that have disappeared. The Santa Fe Historical Society refurbished the cemetery and had a large granite slab engraved with names for whom they have proof of interment. Great-Grandmother Permelia's letters verified the burials of both men.

Rich Smith of Paranormal Investigations of Texas—and author of *Everyplace I Go Is Haunted*—and I corresponded about this graveyard. When I told him about the letter edged in black, he suggested he would place flowers on Lizzie's grave. Rich visited the cemetery and found her gravesite. He quoted excerpts from her letter and also told her I had forwarded it to him. He then placed flowers on Lizzie's grave, as she mentioned in her letter.

Afterward, he turned on his recorder and returned to his car. It was a still night, with no other visitors. After a while, Rich returned for the recorder. When he played it back, there was no static, no sound, until the tape rolled to: "Thank you. Thank you."

Electronic Voice Phenomena is something like making pictures from the clouds. One person is sure he sees a rabbit in that cumulous cloud.

The orbs are not wearing name tags, but. . . .

His friend says, "It does sort of look like a rabbit," when all the time she thought it looked more like a Teddy bear. That's why I'd rather hear EVP for myself first—not hearing what another person thought it sounded like.

Rich sent me the recording. We agree—Lizzie thanked him for the flowers.

On my trip to South Texas, I arrived in Alvin just before dark, where Rich and Mary Smith live. Rich and I drove to Santa Fe, down a narrow road to the Arcadia Evergreen Cemetery. It was a dead end. By that time, early darkness slivered through the clouds and had brought no moon. I had cleverly worn my weather boots, and Rich had a large flashlight. With his knowing where the open gate would be, we tromped through the weeds and, also, many broken trees Hurricane Ike was responsible for. Just because a cemetery has a Texas State Historical Marker, doesn't mean it receives perpetual care. Abandoned cemeteries are tragic.

The evening was so silent, you could almost hear it. Weeds stood tall, and even with Rich's flashlight, we could see few headstones. But I was there for the first time, where my mother once stood as a small child when her father was buried.

On the way to the car, a Tarzan-like vine clutched out at me, sending me to the ground.

Thick, damp wet leaves and wild grasses cushioned my fall. Actually, protecting my cameras held above my head with one hand made it difficult to hold on to the air with the other. But no harm done.

When I later viewed the pictures I shot in the dark, three orbs were clearly visible. If they represent someone buried there, I choose to think Lizzy Romine, Jim Shults, and Andrew Hawkins were acknowledging my visit, someone they never met.

Arcadia Evergreen Cemetery (Private)
Santa Fe, Texas
Oakland off Cemetery Road

GALVESTON, OH GALVESTON

There are some who say Galveston Island is entirely haunted. Houses, castles, depots, and hotels have mysterious occurrences that some would like to forget. Incidents remain in the memories of others, as weird experiences that have no explanation.

In 1785, when Jose de Evia chartered the Texas coast, he named Galveston Bay in honor of the viceroy of Mexico, Bernardo de Galvez. Jean LaFitte's pirate camp occupied the site for five years, until the United States forced him to vacate in 1821. In 1830, Mexico established a customs house as a port of entry. The harbor served for the Texas Navy during the Revolution, and as the Texas government's last position of retreat.

Canadian Michael B. Ménard bought land for $50,000 from the Austin Colony to establish the city of Galveston. After he ran out of funds, he approached a group of moneyed and influential men to help. One was Gail Borden Jr., publisher of *The Telegraph* and *Texas Register*, as well as inventor of condensed milk. Two others were Thomas F. McKinney, a cotton trader, and Samuel May Williams, a successful merchant and former secretary to Stephen F. Austin.

Galveston was once home to more millionaires than any other city in the United States. It was rich—the "Wall Street of the Southwest"—receiving the title mainly because of its being a major exporter of cotton and grain. Such a title gave it a feeling of confidence. So how could a mere hurricane threat of 1900 possibly be of major consequence? They did not build a seawall. The citizens soon realized what a masterful error they had made.

Subsequently, they constructed a seventeen-foot seawall, sure to prevent another such catastrophe. But Galveston still had not recovered. It thrived as a center for prostitution and gambling until the Texas Rangers closed down the activities in 1957. There may still be old slot machines buried in the Gulf, where the Rangers tossed them.

In a *New York Times* article of October 31, 1982, "A 19th-century Island City," Robert Rheinhold wrote, "By the turn of the century, when people were still shooting each other in most other parts of Texas, Galveston had an opera house, a medical school, the first electric lights and the first country club and golf course in Texas."

Galveston Island is a Mecca for tourists and vacationers, with special places to envelop your eyes and even more to do.

The meaning of bumper-to-bumper traffic became clear the early morning I drove into Galveston on Broadway Boulevard, six weeks after Hurricane Ike devastated the island. It occurred to me workers were driving in to repair businesses, homes, roofs, and to install glass in gaping windows. Where had all the fences gone?

We had heard of the destruction from the media and from families who lived there, what it was like to be left with nothing. Both *The Galveston Daily News* and Google Alerts kept the public updated on the Internet as to the island's progress. The Historical Foundation was kind enough to send me regular reports during the clean-up process—the resurrection of a great city.

We also learned of the help, monetary and otherwise, given by individuals throughout the state.

Although it would take years for normalcy to return to Galveston, an amazing fete had been accomplished in so short a time after the most vicious Texas storm since 1900.

NICARAGUA SMITH

As the story goes, the ghost of Nicaragua Smith cries out at night. If he knew I was going to write about him, he might have at least called to me, even though it was a sunny afternoon.

January 8th is a date Thomas Smith, AKA Nicaragua Smith, will surely remember from 1862 throughout eternity. That was the day he died—driven to his gravesite where the executioners ended his last day on earth.

During the 1850s, William Walker, a soldier of fortune and self-styled revolutionary from Tennessee, set ship to Nicaragua, with the ambition of taking it over. He had previously invaded Mexico and was familiar with the "how-to" process. Smith had been with Walker on his filibustering expedition against Nicaragua, which is where his nickname originated. He developed a reputation no one would want tattooed on his forehead. Nevertheless, Smith managed to escape the hands of justice.

Around 1861, he drifted to New Orleans and South Texas. Because he had no money, he separated various businesses and individuals from theirs. After Captain N. B. Yard arrested him, Smith found himself on a steamboat to Houston. "Don't come back to Galveston, y'hear?"

Of course, going back to Galveston did enter his mind. Perhaps out of some loyalty or a desire for food on the table, he joined the Confederate artillery battery. It wasn't to his liking, not that he expected it would be. So he chose a particularly dark night to steal a small boat. He rowed out to the Union blockader, where he surrendered and was promptly dispatched as a prisoner of war to New Orleans. He told the Union authorities he was born in the north and favored the Union. They bought his story. Nicaragua had traded sides in a matter of days.

On October 4, 1862, the Union Navy captured Galveston.

Major General John. B. Mcgruder, appointed Confederate commander of military forces in Texas on November 29, had as his sole mission, to recapture the city.

At 3:00 in the morning on New Year's Day, 1863, four Confederate gunboats steered into Galveston Bay. They opened fire just before dawn. Union forces included three companies of the 42nd Massachusetts Volunteer Infantry Regiment.

Colonel Joseph J. Cook, in command on the island, failed to seize the wharf because ladders provided for his men were not long enough. The combined Confederate Army and Navy forces, led by Mcgruder, launched an assault and returned the city of Galveston to the Confederacy.

Under Colonel Davis's command, the Federal transport, *Cambria*, carrying regiments, equipment and heavy guns, dropped anchor. Davis knew nothing of the recapture of Galveston the day before. As a result, the captain raised the blue and white "Blue Peter" flag, which signaled to take a pilot onboard. When no bar pilot appeared, Davis sent a yawl of men to inform those on shore of the transport's arrival. And who commanded the craft? Nicaragua Smith.

When they reached shore, recognition of Smith was quick. No matter he had been with Walker in his filibustering expedition against Nicaragua. He was now on the side of the Union.

The Confederates thought to capture the fleet, so they sent out men dressed in federal uniforms to conduct the enemy in. But when they arrived, the signals and salutes raised suspicion. After questioning, the Union confirmed their distrust and bargained to exchange another man for Nicaragua Smith . . . Apparently not enough bargaining power. The Cambria returned in haste to New Orleans.

Nicaragua received a court-martial and a guilty verdict of "inexcusable desertion." His sentence of death by firing squad would be carried out the following day.

History tells us Nicaragua rode in the wagon which carried his coffin to his burial site in Galveston's Old City Cemetery. Standing in front of the "twelve messengers of death," the lieutenant in charge asked him if he had any last message. His answer was "Yes," followed by a statement that won't be printed here (even if I knew it). He asked to be buried face downward, for reasons of which only he was aware.

It will soon be the 150th anniversary of his death. When you drive by the cemetery on the cloudy, moonless night of January 8th—of any year, listen carefully. The eerie screams may come from there or from the vaporous mists of the ocean. They say Smith is cursing the firing squad, or perhaps it's his death throes from the bullets. I don't know what time of night, but people say they've heard the cries.

There is something about Nicaragua Smith's life that carries a swashbuckling flare, not at all like Jean Lafitte, but as a flamboyant adventurer. Sure, he tried to burn down Galveston more than twice, but still, with a name like Nicaragua . . . .

Old City Cemetery
Between 40th and 43rd at Avenue K
Galveston, Texas 77550

Nicaragua doesn't call out during the day.

One Step at a Time

My life is now ended
Cease mourning for me
Closed be the morrow
The future none see.

Were Clara Ménard, adopted daughter of Michel B. Ménard, to have written the above, would there have been no mourning? When she and her sister, Helen, were young, Clara fell down the long flight of stairs in their impressive six-columned home. She broke her neck in the tragic fall . . . and someone is haunting Ménard Manor.

The girls' stepfather was born near Montreal in 1805. At the age of fourteen, he worked with John Jacob Astor in the fur-trading business. As a young man, he migrated to Nacogdoches and realized the value of speculating land in Texas. With his purchase of 4,600 acres in 1836, he helped incorporate the city of Galveston and was a signer of the Texas Declaration of Independence.

Good fortune may have followed him many years in the business world, but tragedy stayed close in his marital life. His first wife, Dianne LeClerc, died of cholera in 1833 en route to Texas. Four years later, he married Catherine Maxwell, his cousin, and began building a house. She died of "childbed fever" the following summer. Mary Jane Clemens Riddle, the third Mrs. Ménard, died four years after that, at thirty-three. Two years later, Michel married a widow, Rebecca Mary Bass. Rebecca had two daughters, Helen and Clara, from a previous marriage.

The splendid house, known as "The Oaks," stood on ten acres of sandy soil. At the time, it was located a distance from town, in order to avoid stale air of the city.

In 1856, Michel Ménard died of cancer at the age of fifty-one. His remaining family lived in the house over twenty years until police chief Edwin N. Ketchum purchased it, re-naming the house "Old Chaparral." Soon, weeds and overgrowth had transformed the once-beautiful estate into an eyesore.

The home changed hands more than once during the next decades, and eventually became abandoned. The crumbling structure was a refuge for transients and drug dealers. In 1994, almost on the eve of demolition, Fred and Pat Burns purchased the house and resolved to bring it back to its original beauty. It took years of research and reconstruction, but knowing they planned to live there, it was worth the effort.

Originally, Ménard had the house built in the east, then shipped it piece by piece to Galveston. The house's sturdy construction pays tribute to its lumber used as ship's ballast in 1838. Mr. and Mrs. Burns furnished it with glorious antiques and accessories. After the renovation, they decided to give the home to the Galveston Historical Foundation for a museum.

Since it is the oldest surviving house in Galveston, perhaps its ghosts are also the oldest.

A person of interest in our story is Rebecca Jane, Michel Ménard's widow. At a party one evening, journalist and Colonel John Sidney Thrasher met Rebecca, wooed, won, and married her in 1860. People considered him an adventurer and somewhat of a womanizer. He wanted to put the Ménard property in his name, which, possibly was not in his wife's best interest. (At the time, Rebecca's estate was valued at $50,000.) They eventually moved to Georgia for the health of Rebecca and Michel's fourteen-year-old son, Doswell, who had epilepsy.

Her husband returned to Texas and would send her money. Rebecca was in failing health and distraught over the death of her daughter,

The Ménard House.

Clara, on September 24, 1864. Since John had not contacted her in two months, she feared he was dead. She asked if her Galveston property could be mortgaged so she could have the funds. It apparently did not go into John's name. Eventually, she learned funds were available to her "on her order." John brought his family back to Galveston in 1865.

I digressed into genealogy there for a moment, but if the long-time legend is true that Clara, as a young girl, fell down the stairs and broke her neck in the mansion, how could she die as a young adult in Georgia in 1864? According to the archives of Notre Dame, the latter is fact.

Still, back in the mansion, fleeting glimpses of a masculine apparition on the premises have been minimal. Michel had worked so hard for what he had, it seems plausible he would want to keep tabs on the renovated mansion.

Incidents involving womanly apparitions, however, have occurred more often. Objects move and turn up in other places. It's as if someone prefers a rose bowl on an end table rather than on a console. Such poltergeist activity is usually—not always—expected from youngsters.

Several people have vowed they've seen a mysterious woman in the house through the years. Could she be Diane? But Diane didn't live to see the mansion. Catherine didn't live there long enough to think of it as home. Mary Jane couldn't have really enjoyed it during her short life as mistress of "The Oaks." She may, however, have wanted to stay around longer before crossing into the light. And of course, Rebecca remarried, and even though they eventually moved out of state, perhaps she loved the house enough to return.

What about young Clara? Legend says she fell down the stairs and landed by the steps at the entryway. It is at this very spot people feel the most eerie prescience. Could it have been Clara's sister who actually fell down the stairs? (Only a theory.) In research, I have found nothing about Helen since Michel Ménard adopted her.

With all those possibilities, who is more likely the ghost of Ménard Mansion? Even though we think we chose the right one, it isn't a scratch off. We may never know the answer.

Michel B. Ménard Home
1605 33rd Street
Galveston, Texas 77550
For Information: 409-762-3933

The Gingerbread House

No ghosts left breadcrumbs here. Actually, the name comes from its architecture. With fourteen rooms of antiques and accessories in the Gingerbread House, a ghost would have many places to wander.

Shadowy forms move about the grounds of what was once the Van Alstyne's home. The family came from the Netherlands to New York. In 1841, William Van Alstyne ventured to Texas. In many nineteenth-century success stories, men came from the east to seek their fortunes. So far, I haven't run across many men of that time period leaving Texas to make their fortunes in the east.

Van Alstyne stopped in Houston and went into business in a big way. He built the town's first three-story building and was responsible for bringing the first train to Texas. He married Maria Wright and started a family. When their son, Albert, was grown, he moved to Galveston to make his own personal fortune. A Texas town was his namesake.

The renowned Nicholas J. Clayton designed the Van Alstyne house in Houston—no report of its having been haunted. After Albert married Catherine Stone Lufkin (the Texas town of the same name, founded circa 1882), Clayton designed their Galveston house. In an early picture, it resembled New York's Flat Iron building—a wedge of a structure. Now, after restoration, and with plants on the wide porches, flowers, and landscaping, it's a comfortable and welcoming show place. How can a ghost not want to meander through the grounds? Owner, Murriah McMaster, has given the interior an original Victorian flavor. The Van Alstynes would be proud.

This grand old house, cream with burgundy and turquoise trim, with upper balcony, has weathered many coastal storms. That it survived the 1900 hurricane is astonishing. But Albert Wright did not build a sugar-candy cottage.

To become more familiar with the possible haunting of the Van Alstyne's old home, Rich Smith, of Paranormal Investigations of Texas, conducted an Electronic Voice Phenomena (EVP) session on the lower floor of the Gingerbread House. He hoped to contact the ghost who had earlier frightened the owner living there. The rain peppered down, resulting in a soft echo sound on the entry canopy.

The voice he recorded sounded angry and dared him to enter the tower. Ready to accept a dare, Rich waited until night and crossed the threshold of the small tower room, turning off the light. It wasn't needed anyway, since lightening flashed across the large front window, a perfect backdrop.

The Gingerbread House.

The ghost apparently lived there himself in the early 1900s, a bad character then, as now, according to Rich. He learned that, as a human, the ghost had held a woman captive during a time in which the house stood vacant.

The ghost threatened Rich, who called him a coward for continuing to bring fear into the house. The EVP ceased, and Rich left the tower. About six months later, he inquired about any more actions by the angry ghost. He learned the ghost had caused no further problems, giving hope he had left for good. Even a ghost wouldn't want to wear the label of a coward.

But if the twilight is just right, it's possible the shadowy figures people have seen will float by. Who knows, one might stroll quite close to you. Some say a womanly form appears in a white organza dress with a ruffle around the hem. She also wears a wide-brimmed organza hat.

The hurricane of September 2008 ripped off boards from the side of the house, broke windows, took away shingles, and destroyed the burgundy awning-covered entrance.

As to the identity of the property's outdoor ghosts, there was no known mysterious event on record to cause the haunting, other than the angry man of the EVP. Not angry at all, if they are the spirits of Albert and Catherine Van Alstyne. They may simply want to return "home" for a visit. If they choose not to enter the house, well, that is one of paranormal's mysteries.

The Gingerbread House
2901 Broadway
Galveston, Texas 77550
409-763-8151

WHO'S IN THE ATTIC NOW?

The 1845 Mott-Witwer House is now privately owned, but the tale is for telling.

Imagine you're trying to fall asleep, but a soft swooshing sound moves across the attic floor above your bed. Those mice again! Or perhaps it's louder, more like squirrels bowling. But it's the other times—noises more like someone moving furniture across the old floorboard. There *is* a room up there, along with the usual storage space, but no one had used it for years.

Neal Witwer knows about the attic. He lived in the Mott House. The attic in this Galveston home has had its share of paranormal activity. A ghost, who spent much time being angry, has resided there. Hopefully, he has crossed over now . . . since his supposed enemy moved away.

Marcus Fulton Mott, born in 1837 in Louisiana, came with his family to Galveston when he was seven. After growing up there, he served as a colonel in the Confederate Army. When the war ended, he returned home to open a law office. The Galveston Artillery Club gave Mott the honorary title of "Captain." He obviously didn't mind the "demotion" in rank, because it was done with affection.

He became a successful businessman and attorney after joining a prestigious law firm with William Ballinger and Thomas Jack. In 1884, he designed a home any ghost would be proud of. For almost sixty years, it has been known as the Mott-Witwer House.

Neal Witwer (anyone into rock 'n roll in Galveston knows his celebrated name—bass player, lead singer, sound engineer) grew up in the 1950s in the house built by Captain Mott. Neal's father, Tommy, was a prominent photographer. His mother, Mary Lou, "secretly" saved enough money during World War II to purchase this 8,500 square foot mansion. It was set up perfectly for his father's studio.

As Neal described it to me, the Victorian mansion had 19-foot ceilings on the lower floor and 25' x 25' bedrooms on the second. Italian terrazzo paved the entry. Just before Neal's family bought the house, the previous owners had transformed the upstairs into six apartments.

When Neal was a toddler, his parents moved into one of the apartments to be closer to the business and, of course, little Neal would be only twenty-seven stair steps away. The house was perfect for them. Neal's older brother, Joseph, said that as a teenager, he had seen Captain Mott's ghost.

Names in this story, other than Mott and the Witwer family, are fictitious. Even before Neal married in 1973 and moved into one of the apartments, their home was so large, his parents didn't mind when he and his friends had a jam session. Jane, the mother of the drummer in Neal's band, was a lovely woman and friend of Mary Lou Witwer and enjoyed listening to the band as much as anyone. Jane was there one evening when an older friend, whom I'll call Ray, a navy veteran, came over. He entered the house from the rear and went into an open door before realizing it was an empty apartment. He then followed the music, which wasn't difficult, through the house's thousands of square feet until he found everybody.

As it happened, Ray needed a place to stay and asked to rent the apartment. After he had been there a while, the house seemed to have taken on an ominous personality. It was almost as if it breathed a churning aura of discontent. Ray began hearing noises. Voices, from the attic.

It turned out that he and Jane began dating and often attended the jam sessions. He finally told Neal there was something strange going on in the house. It was strong enough that he wanted Jane to come by and see what she thought.

At 1:00, they heard a loud dragging sound from the attic. Again at 3:00, 4:00, 5:00, then the clock spun back to 1:00. It couldn't be. It was. Jane hadn't mentioned it before, but later said she had a strange feeling about the house the very first night she was there. They were unnerved by the entire process.

Neal's wife had a friend who was interested in Wicca, so she told Jane about the occurrence and invited her over. She advised them to try to ignore the voices, especially since Jane had a toddler, and the evil spirits might even harm her. The voices were not easy to ignore.

She had mentioned the Ouija board, and they were seriously considering using one.

One night after Ray had fallen into a deep sleep, he abruptly awoke to a voice. "I don't want you here. Get out." The voice repeated the words. Then Ray's mattress pushed up. The voice from the attic said, "Come see me. Come."

Ray didn't resist. He had to see for himself. When he climbed to the attic, a form grabbed and dragged him across the floor to a support post. He felt in a dream, and in three or fours hours, he managed to free himself from this hypnotic grasp and returned downstairs where he called Neal. There was no question something eerie had happened. Rope burns covered Ray's wrists—with no sensible explanation. "What is going on in this house?" he demanded. Neal was as nonplussed as Ray.

At that point, Neal knew only that the large, dark, and yes, scary attic had held a strange fascination for him, even as a small child. Dark places would be frightening to a youngster, but looking back, Neal knew this was a different kind of fright.

They had enough and called in a well-known psychic. They made an appointment for a séance. In the meantime, the area rugs in Ray's room were misplaced. But more than that, a framed photograph lifted from the table and fell onto the floor.

Neal's wife had also begun to express anxiety. When she asked him who the captain was, he was stunned. She could have known nothing about him prior to their marriage. He hadn't even mentioned Captain Mott. But she explained. While sleeping, she became restless and started to get up. But she couldn't. It was as if something were pressing upon her. Then the apparition of a man appeared. "Kathy. Don't be afraid. Katherine, I won't hurt you. Kathleen. Don't be afraid."

He called her by all three names. A day or two later she saw his reflection in her mirror. He said, "I'm Captain Mott. I built this house."

Whenever Neal had investigated the noises they heard from the attic, he found only a dark, dusty area—the usual store-in-the-attic types of things. But his wife had seen the captain up close. He knew he had been in the house, but where, Neal wondered.

And when Neal's little stepdaughter asked her mother who the captain was, her mother thought perhaps she was referring to Captain Kirk, since *Star Trek* was on television about that time. The little girl said, "No, he had a white beard and asked if I wanted to play." But he disappeared.

Has the haunting ceased?

The psychic arrived with a Ouija—none too soon, they thought. Ultimately, they met several times. Ray asked why he was being haunted. The answer astounded him: something to the effect is seems rather bold for a Ouija to relate, but it added that Ray bore a resemblance to Captain Mott's son, Abey.

The spirit controlling the board ordered Ray to go into the attic to find a picture. Was the earlier picture in his room a foreshadowing of the one in the attic? Mustering courage, he entered the dimly-lit place. He didn't know what picture he was looking for. Then he saw one in plain view, as if it waited for him. Returning downstairs with it, he was stunned to see how much he resembled the portrait. Could it be the captain had reason to hate his own son? To take that literally, the captain's spirit must have gained some sort of revenge on the look-alike.

According to that eerie and often considered evil wooden device used during the séance, the psychic asked the captain why he did not like Ray? Or was it his son he did not like? The answer was: "I own this house. My son killed me. He murdered three women and put their bodies in the cistern."

The legend is, Captain Mott's neighbor had a young daughter. Mott's son had killed her and threw her into the cistern. The housekeeper found out and confronted Abey. He had to kill her, too. The third victim was his girlfriend to whom he confessed. When she drew back from him, he was afraid she would tell, and he murdered her as well.

One other significant factor in the tale concerns the survey of a narrow strip of land on the property, the owner of which needed to be located. It had apparently been overlooked in the past. The first female to pass the bar exam in Galveston was handling it, and she engaged a private investigator to try and find out. No luck, so she asked Neal if he knew. He didn't, but the psychic said she would give it a try. The answer was the heir lived in Colorado, and her name was Lou.

Possibly the most bizarre incident was about three nights after the last very loud noise from the attic. Neal's wife was sound asleep. She awoke screaming. "Tell Ray to get the wardrobe trunk out of his room! Tell him!"

Neal, realizing she was panicked, called Ray at once. He had just then brought the trunk down from the attic. It had never been in his room before, but somehow, Neal's wife knew it was there. With all that had gone on in the past, Ray quickly took it into the yard and left it. The strange thing was, when they later inspected the trunk, it was empty. Perhaps back then if they'd had DNA. . . .

They never found the bodies in the cistern. If an undiscovered well exists it may be covered with decades of soil.

At the advice of a parapsychologist, the séances stopped.

The story is Captain Mott suffered a fatal accident in a fall from a streetcar in 1906. So, did the son push him? Records tell us, however, that he died at home. Even though Galveston had a fine, first hospital in Texas, if they couldn't save him, they may have sent him home to die.

Soon, Neal's marriage failed. Ray also left Galveston for North Texas. Hopefully, in time, he erased the experiences from his memory bank, or at least, had no dreams about them.

One-story businesses now stand between the curb and the house, which is painted yellow. The large white-frame upper portion shows the single window—the attic room.

Marcus Fulton Mott was not unfriendly in life. He was a remarkable man, both as a Colonel and as an eminent attorney. According to the Ouija, the spirit would not leave until somebody found the bodies. But no one has reported mysterious sounds coming from the attic for a long time. Of course, perhaps no one is listening.

The case rests.

> Mott-Witwer House (Private Residence)
> 1117-1121 Tremont Street
> Galveston, Texas 77550

Hotel Galvez

Galveston desperately needed a large hotel to replace the one lost in an 1898 fire. Civic leaders were in the planning stage when the 1900 hurricane struck. All the more reason to accelerate their plans. The name Galvez honored Bernardo de Galvez, the Spanish military leader, who led Spanish armies against Britain in the Revolutionary War. The hotel opened in 1911 to music, dancing, and great celebration. But long before the luxurious hotel, the cannabalistic Karankawa and Akoki Indians lived and died on Galveston Island—in the fourteenth century. Spanish explorers later gave it different names, the "Isla de Culebras," ("Isle of Snakes") and "Malhado, the "Isle of Doom." "Galveston" was the name Jose de Evia gave to the area near the mouth of the river more than two centuries later.

The Galvez is located on the site where the Electric Pavilion (a jazz hot-spot), the Beach Hotel, and Pagoda Bathhouse once stood. *Hotel*

Monthly lists it as one of the "best arranged and most richly furnished seaside hotels in America." It is in the National Register of Historic Places.

James Stewart, Frank Sinatra, Dwight Eisenhower, and Teddy Roosevelt have all checked into this lavish hotel with a breathtaking view of the Gulf.

The picture shown is six weeks after Ike, and the roof is receiving repairs. The palm trees are a little sad. When I returned to Galveston in April 2009, a giant orange boom sat at the entrance, still contributing to rooftop repairs.

Reports of the paranormal in the Galvez Hotel began decades ago. After guests had dinner or partied and retired to their rooms, the staff reported the hotel quiet, the lobby and imposing loggia with an ethereal atmosphere. There are innumerable reasons for the ghostly activity.

A portrait of Bernardo de Galvez hangs on the wall at the end of a long hall in the hotel. Standing in front of the portrait, you may notice

his piercing brown eyes staring at you. Take a step, then turn back quickly. His haunting eyes will still be on you.

Within the last few years the hotel and its 224 deluxe guest rooms have undergone a $9-million restoration in keeping with its Victorian heritage. "The Queen of the Gulf" deserves its name and reputation.

Legends of long ago change through the years, sometimes from person to person and from one telling to the next. The following two accounts are similar.

The Turrets

The turrets atop the Galvez play an important part in this tale. A young bride-to-be checked into Room 500 (some say 505) and waited for her fiancé to return from the sea. Wanting a better view, she walked up the steps to one of the turrets in order to see her sweetheart's ship appear on the horizon. She became nervous after so long a time. Eventually, she received the tragic news his ship had sunk. A few passengers survived, but her sweetheart's name was not on the list.

Dispirited and still hoping the message was in error, she patiently waited. After all hope waned, she again went to the turret where she hanged herself. If she had only waited longer. The message had indeed erred, and her fiancé returned. The young man left in despair, but his fiancée's spirit remained. Some have reported seeing her apparition and have heard quiet, lingering sobs.

An occurrence since that time is a light in the turret, which often comes on when no one is there. Guests have reported seeing the light even though there is reportedly no electrical connection.

Room 500

Some guests who have stayed in Room 500 felt uneasy, as if someone were sharing the room—someone who hadn't checked in. The maids have felt the same presence while preparing for the next guests.

Another account is of a young couple who married in 1911 and chose the Galvez for their honeymoon. After checking in, they went to their room—500. The groom carried his petite bride over the threshold, a 2,000-year-old tradition.

Once inside, they realized the bellboy had not brought up their luggage. The groom did not want to leave his bride but decided to go downstairs to check.

After waiting for some time, the bride became alarmed when her husband failed to return. She hastened to see about him. When she entered the large lobby, she couldn't help seeing a crowd gathered around a man on the floor. With a sudden feeling of apprehension, she rushed

The young woman watched from the turret for her sweetheart's ship.

over to see what had happened. She pushed through the chattering crowd. Someone was trying to revive him and called for a doctor. She could scarcely believe her eyes.

At first she thought her husband had fallen down the stairs, until she knelt by his side. As if a knife had been plunged into her heart, she realized he was dead. But there was no visible reason. Demoralized, she allowed a member of the staff to escort her back to her room. When alone and unable to bear the tragedy, she committed suicide.

Present employees, especially ones who have worked in the Galvez the longest, don't always react anymore to the sudden cold wisps of air they identify as the bride's spirit. Occasionally when a worker needs to repair something in Room 500, any battery-operated implement or electrical equipment will malfunction.

One bizarre incident occurred when a guest told management his room swayed. Accommodating, the night clerk provided him another room. Either it really did sway or he had one margarita too many. Nevertheless, he made no more complaints.

The Swimming Pool

The beautiful swimming pool has a more contemporary story all its own. After everyone else had returned inside one evening, a middle-aged couple remained in the pool area, enjoying the atmosphere. They thought they would stay a while longer, so her husband could finish his drink.

The woman lay back in the chaise when she noticed a man standing on the diving board. She thought everyone had left and asked her husband where the man came from. He hadn't seen him before, either.

The figure took a stance, jumped two or three times in preparation, then dived into the water. But he didn't come up. "Do you think he's all right?" the woman asked. They were so intent on scanning the water, neither of them noticed the figure back on the diving board, just like before.

Turning, they saw him again preparing to dive. As he had a clear cut into the water, they paid close attention this time. He never surfaced. The husband went inside to report a possible tragedy, while his wife remained at the pool, watching.

Security verified no one was in the pool. The wife assured everyone her husband had just two drinks, and she, only one. They returned to their room, knowing they witnessed a phenomenon—just what, they were never certain.

Hunting the Ghosts

The Galveston Ghosthunters investigated the Galvez and asked to stay in the alleged haunted room. They were there at a time when the fifth floor was undergoing renovation, but 500 was still available, and the manager allowed them to stay in it. If asked, the staff will gladly tell you what they know. Early in 2009, Room 501 showed paranormal activity for at least one paranormal group.

During the night, doors all along the hall slammed repeatedly. When someone investigated, all was quiet, but only temporarily. Some think the "Lovelorn Lady" is still searching for her husband in each room and slams the door when he's not there.

Once the group arrived at the fifth floor, they agreed the mood "grew darker." One of the members noted the batteries in her camera kept dying—not uncommon in haunted places, or even in supposed un-haunted places where a spirit is present.

Other eerie incidents have occurred, especially those causing people to feel someone was watching them, or the sudden swirl of cold air. No one ever said Señor Bernardo de Galvez couldn't step down from the gold picture frame and wander around the hotel.

The Galveston and Texas Historical Center estimated between 6,000 and 8,000 people died in the 1900 storm. Hundreds of victims washed ashore, buried beneath the sand on which the Galvez Hotel now stands.

Called an island of snakes over 600 years ago, pirates, mysterious deaths, suicides—not to forget cannibalistic Karankawas, what better foreshadowing to a haunted island.

The Galvez loggia.

Galvez Hotel
2024 Seawall Boulevard
Galveston, Texas 77550
409-765-7721
www.galveston.com/galvez/

THE HOTEL IN THE WATER

Who, or what, roams the seventh floor of the Flagship Hotel in Galveston?

The Flagship Hotel stemmed from the city's plan for a 1912 Pleasure Pier amusement park like that of Atlantic City. Promoters kept it on the table until 1931, when they drew up the plans. World War II intervened, however, and the project opened in 1948, complete with a ballroom, theatre, T-Head fishing pier, and snack bar.

The entire plan was overly-ambitious and subsequently, it failed when Galveston defaulted on payments. In 1963, Houston financier, James E. Lyon, could see the future for a hotel on the four-block-long pier. Many negotiations later, Lyons built the 240-room Flagship Hotel, which opened in 1965.

There is no other hotel in North America like it. First, it was built on a historic pier 1,000 feet off Galveston Island—right over the Gulf of Mexico. The drive from the island to the pier is a concrete ramp leading to the entry. Park your car either close and parallel to the hotel, or if there is no space, back . . . no, let's forward your car to the edge . . . and engage your emergency brake.

No matter where your guest room is, water is your view as far as you can see.

But something you may never see is the reported ghost, who wanders the seventh floor.

In the case of a revenant, I never know whether to call it a *which* or a *who*. Since the ghost actually represents a person, let's go with "who." Hotel guests who have seen this apparition say it seems to be a real person. Actually, they are certain up until he disappears through a wall or walks through an un-open door.

During Hurricane Ike, the hotel endured structural damage when the piers weakened. One partial corner fell from north end of the building. The only way to the Flagship is via a concrete ramp from the island. The fierce water crumbled it, leaving eleven employees stranded in the hotel. Help came to their rescue, all uninjured, with the manager the last to leave.

There was major damage at the Flagship Hotel just after Hurricane IKE.

The Flagship Hotel was in desperate need of repair, even before Hurricane Ike. The report now is the owners might restore it, or more likely, will sell it for demolition or to "serious" buyers, who are considering replacing it with a "pleasure pier" with amusement rides. The ghosts will be patient.

The Flagship Hotel
Seawall Boulevard
Galveston, Texas 77550

ONE MAN'S CASTLE IS ANOTHER MAN'S PALACE

The Bishop's Palace was one of the first historical homes to reopen after Hurricane Ike's damage—its second extraordinary survival of a great storm.

The Library of Congress recognizes The Bishop's Palace in Galveston as one of the fourteen most representative Victorian structures in the nation. With a review like that, no wonder a few ghosts delight in wandering about its luxurious interior.

The story of Walter Gresham is as historical as the house he built. Born in 1841 in Virginia, the son of Edward Gresham and Isabella Mann graduated from the University of Virginia in 1863 and served as a colonel in the Confederacy. After the Civil War dissipated the family fortunes, he moved to Galveston with five dollars to his name. He became successful in his law practice, and in 1868, married his cousin, Josephine Carey Mann.

Gresham served as district attorney for the Galveston judicial district and was a man of many careers. Aside from his elections to multiple political offices, including serving in the House of Representatives and the Fifty-third Congress, he was a stockholder and attorney for the Gulf, Colorado, and Santa Fe Railway. With all these activities, he never stopped working for the benefit of the city.

After accruing great wealth, in 1877, he commissioned the renowned architect, Irish-born Galveston resident, Nicholas J. Clayton, to build a home for him and his wife. Clayton apparently had carte blanche in his endeavor. Using exotic woods, he created a masterpiece, with no equal west of New York. It contained an intricately carved wooden staircase, stained glass windows, sculptures, nine turrets, and bronze dragons. The list goes on: Massive sliding wooden doors, both sides matching the rooms they face, according to "Texas Less Traveled." A $250,000 cost of such a residence sounds reasonable, even for nineteenth-century Texas. The Greshams formally opened their palatial "Gresham's Castle" on January 1, 1893.

The disastrous flood of 1900 destroyed thousands of buildings all around the castle, but when waters subsided, it still stood like a fortress, built of steel, granite, and stone. Over 600 people flocked to it for sanctuary.

Walter Gresham died November 6, 1920. Three years later the Galveston-Houston Diocese of the Catholic Church bought the residence for $40,500, quite a drop from its original cost. The Diocese purchased it for their offices and the residence of Bishop Christopher Byrne, the only bishop who ever lived there. From that time on, its official name became "The Bishop's Palace." After Byrne's death in 1950, the palace remained vacant.

Thirteen years later, the Catholic Church opened it as a museum. Realizing it was possibly haunted came as a surprise to the staff. It is, however, Galveston's best-known paranormal building and a favorite of Dash Beardsley's "Ghost Tours of Galveston Island."

Many people, who believe they know beyond a shadow of a ghost, have identified the spirits of the Palace. The revenant of Walter Gresham seems to be the most probable. Josephine Gresham was an artist and loved the palatial home. She painted the faces of their nine children on cherubs on the high ceilings. She may be a regular visitor today, admiring her work and musing over her offspring.

Of course, Josephine hadn't lived there for almost thirteen years before her death in 1933, but she could easily cherish it to the extent she returns. Some have seen the apparition of a woman gracefully ascend the carved staircase.

The Bishop Byrne lived in the palace for almost thirty years, about the same length of time as Walter Gresham. Many people believe it is Gresham's spirit that returns, or perhaps he never left.

As time progressed, tiles fell from the elaborate roof of the structural masterpiece and decay took over. The situation became dangerous. As Houston Mayor Lyda Ann Thomas said, "Historical Galveston would not be the same without this crown jewel of the late 19th-century architecture."

As of December 2007, the Galveston Historical Foundation accepted responsibility of the daily operation and maintenance of Bishop's Palace. The Archdiocese retains ownership.

The impressive Bishop's Palace.

Through the years, so many visitors have reported cold spots, the feeling of being watched, and of hearing whispers, the belief the palace is haunted seems even more plausible.

Don't wander off. A tour group that stays together . . . is safer.

The Bishop's Palace
1402 Broadway Street
Galveston, Texas 775507
For Information: 409-762-2475

QUEEN ANNE BED AND BREAKFAST

The Queen Anne Bed and Breakfast is special—light blue with white trim, second-floor balcony, charming, comfortable, even suitable for small weddings.

No one knows the identity of the ghost who wanders through the halls. The great flood of 1900 occurred only five years before the construction of this home. But still, an earlier lost spirit may have wandered in, found the house to its liking, and simply remained.

George B. Stowe, renowned architect of impressive dwellings, designed the home for businessman James J. Davis and his family. Davis, in his late thirties when he built the house, died seventeen years after its completion in 1905. Mrs. Davis continued to live there, but ultimately, sold it to the First Methodist Church across the street.

The Methodists retained ownership for over twenty years, then it changed hands twice before current owners took over. Subsequently, the church moved to a larger location.

Ron and Jackie Metzger purchased the Davis home in 1998. The house, after being vacant for many years, fell into disrepair. The Metzgers visualized its potential, restored it, and opened the Queen Anne Bed and Breakfast two years later. While they lived there, they realized tenants of an ethereal nature were non-paying guests. Who could know for sure what caused the metaphysical occurrences? With others living in the house in intervening years, it could be any spirit at all.

With no visible assistance, a rocking chair moves on its own. Objects fly from one place to another. Unaccountable sounds seem to sigh from the woodwork. The Metzgers heard footsteps coming from various parts of the house or on occasion, from the stairway. Shadows resembled human forms but would stay only an instant, disappearing before Jackie or Ron could get close.

One evening, Jackie went upstairs to make a room ready for the next day. After finishing, she turned off the lights and returned downstairs. The next morning, she was stunned to see a large red circle on the carpet just outside the bedroom door. She and her husband had no clue as to what caused it. They called in a carpet-cleaning company. "Bizarre" seemed to be the correct description. The red spot returned and left more than once, but much later, it disappeared entirely.

There are new owners at the Queen Ann at this time. With its spacious rooms, Victorian décor, and hospitality they have offered, no wonder it received one of ten national "Best Overall" awards from BedandBreakfast.com, the leading online bed and breakfast directory, worldwide.

A few weeks after Hurricane Ike struck, the exterior of the house still looked inviting, because of quick clean-up. Red and white caladiums bordered the front in springtime, but only hedges and greenery graced the front area when I was there. During the flood, water covered the dozen steps to the porch and rushed into the house. The window of a ground-level 500-square-foot suite opened like a floodgate.

It was not until Ike left the island that anyone knew the house's structural qualities. After September 2008, the house stood erect. I'd planned to stay at the Queen Anne the week before the hurricane, because its website appealed to me. Besides, I like B&Bs, especially haunted ones. I decided to wait a couple weeks, a decision I regretted—at the time.

Unfortunately, the Queen Ann closed after the hurricane—hopefully, only temporarily. The spirit or spirits lived in the house before it was a Bed and Breakfast. There's no reason to believe they left just because it closed to worldly guests.

> Queen Anne Bed and Breakfast
> 1915 Sealy Street
> Galveston, Texas 77550

SAMUEL M. WILLIAMS HOME

Samuel M. Williams, son of Howell and Dorothy (Wheat) Williams, was born October 4, 1795, in Providence, Rhode Island. He was a man who developed much business acumen.

Perhaps too much, for he was a long way from winning a popularity contest, or so history tells us.

As a young teenager, he worked for his uncle in his general store, where he learned the mechanics of business. He moved on to various firms, and at twenty, he moved down to New Orleans. A man on the move, and as such, he learned to speak several languages.

Williams soon met Stephen F. Austin, and by the age of thirty, was his new friend's secretary, maintaining records, maps—all intricate phases of business that would help Austin's colony succeed. Austin trusted him to "take care of business" while he went to Mexico.

In 1829, Williams married Sarah Scott and built a home for her in Galveston. A white-framed house with dormers and an additional room on the top, much like an over-sized cupola, with a balcony.

During IKE, the water line was past the front door at the Queen Anne.

The unfortunate occurred. Mexicans imprisoned Austin without charges. Little did he know that while he was in prison for twenty-eight months, Williams would be at play—spending money of his own as if he had much more, plus being involved in fraudulent land deals with Austin's money.

Williams did have a good side to his character. With Thomas McKinney, he opened the state's first bank. The two risked their lives to purchase ships for the Texas Navy. According to historian Jeff Carroll, who has studied this phase of Texas history in depth, Williams called in payment from Austin's colonists, to whom Austin had previously given freely. This did not seem to concern Williams, as he probably thought Austin would remain in prison forever. He continued in land speculations and banking services, becoming wealthy via his own expertise and others' misfortune.

A curious thing, however, is Williams had this great opportunity to excel, and he obviously was trying to obtain his benefactor's release. After Austin returned, he learned full well what Williams had done and dismissed him as a friend. It's hard to believe he died penniless, not even owning his own home.

They say an apparition walks around the cupola.

Samuel Williams' shady business dealings continued, as if he anxiously waited for tardy bank loans. Foreclosures are not new. He died in 1858. What goes around . . . comes falling down. At least, he left his house, one of the oldest structures on the Island.

Without his leaving a will, his four surviving children sold the house to Philip Tucker, whose family sold it in 1953 to the Historical Foundation. Now as far is known, the Tuckers never reported any paranormal activity. Doesn't mean there wasn't any. Some people ignore such things, believing they never happened—just a tree limb hitting against the roof, or a woodpecker under the eaves.

But what has happened since then has caused people to take interest. First, more than a few people have said they felt a presence when they toured the house. Two have said they felt a great shortness of breath. Granted, that experience is common to allegedly haunted places.

In Lisa Farwell's book, *Haunted Texas Vacations*, she mentions a neighbor who periodically checked on the house. This was before the Historical Foundation took it over. When the neighbor entered, he noticed still-glowing embers in the fireplace and knew for a fact no one could have entered the house. That was evidence enough for him to believe a ghost had warmed himself by the fireplace. The Tuckers had all apparently "crossed over" later with no problem.

The most intriguing comment concerns the figure, which witnesses have said moves around on that little balcony on top of the house. Remember, the copula thing? The apparition moves back and forth from one end of the short balcony to the other. It's definitely not a shadow cast from a passing car. As I wanted to see for myself, I stood outside, looking up for more time than I'd planned to spend. The power of suggestion, perhaps, but I do believe I saw such a shadowy figure. I must say it rather startled me.

At that point, I went in for the tour, anxious to go upstairs to see if someone might still be there. But the outer door stays locked—no human could have been on the balcony.

For the illegal things ol' Samuel had responsibility for and ending up the way he did . . . I don't mean just dead . . . perhaps he does return, hoping to regain his wealth.

The Samuel M. Williams House
3601 Avenue P
Galveston, Texas 77550
409-765-1839

The Phantom of the Opera

The 1894 Grand was one of the early refurbished Galveston treasures to re-open since "Hurricane Ike" played there. Ike didn't get good reviews. The interior flooded, the orchestra pit a swimming pool. Scaffolding, paint, electricians, new flooring—all in order of operation when I visited to see my favorite entertainment spot in Galveston.

Charles Francis Coghlan, famous actor and playwright of the 1800s, plays a role in this story. Coghlan founded the Fortune Bay Actor's Colony on Prince Edward Island off Canadian shores. He was America's top leading man of his time. Keep that thought. We'll come back to it.

Galveston's Grand 1894 Opera House was originally an old icehouse, built in 1850 and the first brick building on Postoffice Street. Later, businesses occupied its three floors until the Civil War. Afterward, people looked for entertainment to help bring back normalcy. The building opened as the Varieties Theatre.

When the 1890s rolled around, the theatre had seen its last performance. Henry Greenwall, a theatrical entrepreneur, and several Galveston businessmen had the structure demolished. With a scenic designer and architect, they designed the 1894 Grand Opera House of Galveston. They had undertaken the momentous task of supporting the arts in Galveston and raised $100,000 to construct their project. The opening performance was *The Daughters of Eve*, starring Marie Wainwright.

The opera house got off to a roaring start, and then the darkest day arrived. The 1900 hurricane destroyed the east wall and the entrance's overhang. Upon reflection, the entire building could have been carried away. But in three years, it was back in operation with vaudeville acts, touring companies, and one-reel motion pictures.

Now, for Charles Francis Coghlan: When descendants of witnesses to the horrific 1900 storm listen to stories passed down, perhaps this one stands at the top of the list. Legend is, Irish-born Coghlan achieved fame in the late 1800s. He was a Shakespearean actor, a playwright, and leading man. In 1899, he was touring with his daughter in the play, *The Royal Box*, which he had written. Coghlan, a man of good looks and stature, had an upcoming performance of *Hamlet*, at the Grand Opera House.

There are varied reports of what happened next, most of which were printed in Texas newspapers, as well as in the East. During a performance of "Hamlet," on November 27, 1899, Charles Coghlan dropped dead.

Another report stated he was stricken with gastritis as soon as he arrived in the city, and an understudy took over for him, at least for one night. But others reports agree, Coghlan died while performing. He had been staying at The Tremont during his time.

In the *Galveston Daily News* of November 29, 1899, his widow planned to have his remains cremated, according to his wishes. Since there was no crematorium nearby, she would accompany his body back to New York for cremation. This never happened, because her daughter, Gertrude, was gravely ill. Mrs. Coghlan made a rushed trip back home.

His body lay in a vault at Levy Brothers Funeral Home at Lakeview Cemetery until Mrs. Coghlan could make arrangements for transferal to the East Coast.

During the 1900 flood over a year later, Coghlan's coffin tore loose in the cemetery and was carried out to sea. Hundreds of others washed away. Cemetery records show his remains were lost during the Great Storm. In 1907, *The Daily News* confirmed it as fact.

Hence, the legend begins.

In 1908, according to www.Farshores.org, Charles Coghlan's coffin drifted from Galveston to the Gulf Stream, where it drifted north, until the "tide bore it into the Gulf of St. Lawrence, where it came ashore not far from his home," in St. Edward Island, Canada.

The story caught on to the extent that authors, newspapers, and Robert L. Ripley picked it up for "Believe It or Not" in 1927. Lilly Langtry wrote this end was predicted for him by a crystal-gazer when he was a young man. *The Theatre Magazine* wrote that on his last departure from St. Edward, he announced, "I will return come hell and high water."

His daughter, Gertrude Pitou, had not heard the story before reading it in Ripley's "Believe It or Not." She had hired people for thousands of dollars to search for her father's remains.

According to *The Galveston Daily News*, when she asked *The Evening Post* to find out where Ripley's information came from, she learned he had cited published memoirs of two of Coghlan's fellow thespians as his source.

Many believe the legend of the floating coffin falls into the category of "Legends Won't Die." Still, there are those who remain fervent to its accuracy.

It's time we found the ghost, but you already know who it is. All the above is foreshadowing. The real shadow is Charles Coghlan himself. Since he never completed his role as Hamlet in the Opera House, he must wonder if they will ever produce it again, and then he could finish his performance. Some have reported seeing a hazy apparition, but with a clear outline, and they assume it is Coghlan. He would occasionally be in the wings watching a performance.

Other times, he simply floats down the farthest aisle, and once I've heard of him in one of the second tier boxes at stage right. The image wears a cape and a hat, Hamlet style.

Spin the reel forward to 1971. The theatre closed for a lengthy renovation, with a gala opening in 1986. Over the years, "The Grand," a spectacular performance hall, presented a roster of celebrities, including Paderewski, Sarah Bernhardt, the Marx Brothers, opera singer Dorothy Kirsten, Helen Hayes to George and Gracie, Dirty Rotten Scoundrels to The Oakridge Boys—the gamut of classical, slapstick, to country.

The Grand Opera House is one of the few theatres of its era still operating in Texas, and in 1993 the 73rd Texas Legislature designated the Grand "The Official Opera House of Texas." With three tiers of boxes on each side of the theatre, it is an authentic opera house. Although the renowned Dame Eva Turner never sang there, I can visualize her opera portrayal of the princess in Puccini's *Turandot* on this stage . . . The Grand is that grand.

The Grand 1894 Opera House
2020 Postoffice Street
Galveston, Texas 77550
409-765-1894
www.thegrand.com

Charles Coghlan appeared at The Grand. *Courtesy of Barb Gatlin*

The Tremont Hotel

Neither fires nor flood will chase the ghosts from The Tremont.

If you are a guest in this elegant hotel, and a hazy apparition rushes past you in the halls, or even appears in your room, it could very well be a salesman named Josh, looking for the money he lost in the 1870s.

The Tremont, an imposing and formal building on The Strand, was first known as the Belmont, on the corner of Tremont and Postoffice Streets. In 1839, it opened with a grand ball honoring the Battle of San Jacinto. Not just anyone attended, considering the cost was fifty dollars in Texas currency or twenty-five dollars in gold.

Perhaps General Sam Houston had the gift of ESP. He made an eerie prediction in his last address, if the South seceded from the Union. He foretold of the "horrors of war" and predicted "fire and rivers of blood."

After 1865, the city rebuilt quickly. When good times visited Galveston, soldiers were accused of thievery, vandalism, and even burning down the old, and first, Tremont. People wanted to claim what they had lost, as well as what belonged to others. The fire consumed The Strand, even after the area had survived the war. Citizens did nothing to rebuild for another five years, leaving most of the charred remnants just as they were.

According to the *Texas Explorer*, several principal Galveston businessmen arranged to bring it back to a grandeur, which would overshadow any other hotel in the South. It opened a year later, but with the grandeur the men had in mind, work stopped at the second floor, for opulence exacted more than their available funds. Burnett & Kilpatrick, a railroad company, took over and completed the hotel.

As old hotels often kept registers, the Tremont shows guests as Rutherford Hayes, Ulysses S. Grant, Benjamin Harrison, and Grover Cleveland. Among other celebrities listed were Buffalo Bill Cody, Clara Barton, Edwin Booth, and the famous ballerina, Anna Pavlova, all of whom stayed in the original hotel.

Eighteen years later, during the hurricane of 1900, citizens heard a storm was coming, but officials had said the low tidal level of the Gulf of Mexico would allow only minimal damage.

Subsequently, visitors and residents hurried to the beaches, now called "haunted," to marvel at the tumultuous waves. They never dreamed of the destruction to follow.

When that realization exploded, they ran for their lives, trampling those who had fallen.

Many scrambled to the Tremont's rooftop, as well as to other buildings, for safety. From that vantage point, they screamed when seeing the overpowering water carry family and friends out to sea.

People drowned trying to reach the four-story building. Husbands who held onto their wives were horrified to see the water sweep them from their grasp. After wind and rain carried away the Tremont's dome, survivors crowded the upper floors, not at all certain the building would not collapse. By night, water stood almost five feet in the first floor of the hotel.

After the hurricane subsided and people cautiously left wherever they had sought refuge, they couldn't believe the thousands of bodies strewn along the streets and beaches—those the waves had not swept into the Gulf.

They buried the corpses as soon as possible, even in their own backyards, whether or not they knew them. Some would never know what befell family members, other than they were undoubtedly dead.

When time became short with the deceased yet unburied, crews dug pits for mass cremation. The city ordered carbolic acid and lime spread in many other graves. Those performing these tasks wore camphor masks and applied disinfectant everywhere they worked. Even now, when new construction takes place, workers discover bones, quite probably from the 1900 catastrophe.

Galveston had a large share of casinos. Gamblers triumphantly spent winnings at the Tremont's ornately carved bar, which was brought to Galveston in 1781.

A gambling salesman named Josh arrived on a sales trip in the late 1870s. No one knew his last name. He checked in at the Tremont. As soon as he learned of the many casinos in town, he decided to try his fortune. It was as if his pockets were full of four-leaf clovers. He won big, so much so, he went straight to the bar to celebrate.

Josh became tipsy and told someone about his winnings. If he wasn't drunk, he simply talked too much. Since it was late and banks were closed, Josh went to his fourth-floor room. He tossed his money on the bed and counted it once more. A knock rattled the door—he shouldn't have opened it. He met the bullet head-on.

The killer stole Josh's money and everything else he had of value.

The following morning, the cleaning woman discovered his body. No one found any clues as to who murdered the salesman. It seems he is still trying to find the killer, the money, or both, long over a century later. Even now, people have claimed to see a well-dressed traveling man carrying a valise, drifting through the halls.

Phantasms, presumedly from the 1900 storm, wander aimlessly throughout the hotel. At least that is an accepted explanation for the hollow footsteps and whispers reported by various guests. The hotel eventually became a casualty to the Great Storm, as well as of the Great Depression. It suffered demolition in 1928, but was no more ready to depart this world than the spirits who dwelt there.

In 1985, George and Cynthia Mitchell acquired the Leon & H. Blum Building and began breathing life into the name, Tremont. The building was once a wholesale dry goods store and proved to be the perfect location for the elegant new hotel.

The old Belmont and Tremont are now one, reconnected on the ground level. The sun slants down from the top of the four-story atrium, through the palm trees to the black and white marble floor. With past battles, deadly storms, and even guests who once stayed at the original Tremont, it isn't surprising people call the hotel haunted.

The bar area of the Tremont has another story. I was told about an incident, which occurred on Valentine's Day in 1998. In preparation for a party, the bartender was arranging vases of roses for the decorations, while the staff watched.

An empty coffee mug sat on the bar. A martini glass was a little farther down from where they all stood. While one of the women was talking, she abruptly stopped and pointed to the glass. The staff stared as the

The Tremont Hotel is back to its original splendor.

glass moved along the bar and fell off the back edge without breaking. It landed at the bartender's feet.

Startled, the barkeeper picked it up and placed a rose in the glass and handed it to the woman. They all had heard the rumors of the salesman's ghost. So thinking the man's spirit might be responsible for the peculiar incident, the woman raised the glass and said, "Mr. Ghost, this is for you."

Other customers sat at the bar, watching. They laughed, a little bewildered.

The coffee mug moved on the bar, the same as the glass. Falling off the back edge, it hit the ice bin but didn't break. It, too, landed at the bartender's feet. She picked it up and asked one of the ladies who already had a rose to put hers in the mug.

This woman really wanted to keep the flower and didn't want to break the stem. With no warning whatsoever, they heard a "whooshing" noise. The head of the rose flew from the stem and dropped to the floor. Curious?

"What matters is what something *is*, not what it's called." A ghost by any other name. . . .

Tremont Hotel
2300 Ship's Mechanic Row
Galveston, Texas 77550
409-763-0300
www.wyndham.com/hotels

Tickets, Please

The last regularly scheduled passenger train left the Galveston Depot on April 11, 1967.

The Santa Fe Railroad purchased the Gulf, Colorado & Santa Fe Railroad and closed the G.C.S.F. offices. The Moody Foundation purchased the amazing Art Deco Union Passenger Depot, saving it from demolition. It's easy to find at 25th & Santa Fe Place—a large cream-colored building just off the Strand, and well-worth visiting, haunted or not.

The central waiting room, built in 1932, is a portion of the building not allocated to offices, businesses, and other organizations. As a museum, it retains the beauty it once had as the train depot.

"Ghosts of Travelers Past." *Courtesy of Virginiae Blackmon*

Renovations completed in 1982 have opened it to the public. Hurricane Ike saw to it that renovations would resume. If you visited the museum prior to 1965, you would recognize where the Harvey House was then. You'd stop at your right to purchase a ticket or walk straight ahead to buy a newspaper to carry with you to the concourses. This museum informs us of railroading in Texas, one of the most informative in the nation.

Rich Smith has investigated the paranormal of Union Station. He carried his EVP recorder and came up with several spirit-messages in the old railroad cars.

The museum also retains spirits of those who once walked across its marble floors.

Intriguing additions to the museum are the lifelike figures in various poses. A couple stands in conversation. Some sit side by side on a bench, with others waiting to catch the next train—should one ever leave. Elliott and Ivan Schwartze, brothers from New York, created the figures. Live models posed for the figures, wrapped in plaster to form a mold. Wires held up their arms, so they could remain in the same position long enough for the plaster to set. If you didn't feel a tendency toward the paranormal when you entered, you would, once you gazed at these eerie "Ghosts of Travelers Past."

Aside from the important story the museum has to tell, that of the "Birth of railroading in Texas," other stories have circulated. One witness vowed to have seen an apparition dressed in a white suit, much like one of the figures, pick up a newspaper and vanish through the closed door as if to board a phantom train.

The interior of the Railroad Museum was destroyed during Hurricane Ike. Desks, bookcases, windows, all furniture, china . . . and the marvelous "Ghosts of Travelers Past," broken in heaps, floating in the water. The museum hopes to be open by spring of 2010, and the ghost figures will be repaired.

> Railroad Museum
> 123 Rosenberg (25th Street)
> Galveston, Texas 77550
> 409-765-5700
> www.galvestonrrmuseum.com

MEDITERRANEAN CHEF

The first time I visited the Mediterranean Chef in October, after Hurricane Ike, I peered into a long rectangular space, completely gutted. The high water fairly well took care of anything below eight feet. But if ghosts can float and/or swim, they weren't in danger. Now if they could only swing a paintbrush and hammer a nail, the restaurant would've opened much sooner.

If a ghost is fond of Grecian food, he has it made in Galveston's Mediterranean Chef. The specialties are Combo Pita Sandwiches, spanakopita, pastishio, salads. What ghost could resist? Fantastic Greek food, and if you're a vegetarian, you couldn't be happier.

The 1920s Galveston had its share of problems, many still left over from the earlier devastating flood. They weren't expecting another. Beginning in March 1920, over 1,500 coastwise longshoremen joined dockworkers in various Gulf and South Atlantic ports in a nationwide walkout. The *Handbook of Texas* explains it thoroughly. The city was in turmoil during that decade. The threat of violence strengthened to the extent the police chief asked Governor William Hobby to send in Texas Rangers to protect non-striking workers.

That wasn't enough. A few months later, the governor declared martial law and sent in 1,000 national guard troops. In July 1920, the governor "suspended the mayor, city commissioners, and police force for failing to maintain the peace and protect citizens." He ordered them to continue performing routine duties but not to enforce penal laws. In the end, the problem seemingly resolved, with the national guard withdrawing September 30, 1920.

That date brings us to October 2 of the same year. The story, from more than one account, is a robber followed an early version of an armored car, to the bank at 2402 Strand Street. When the guard exited the vehicle, carrying the money inside, the robber drew out his gun and attempted to hold him up. The guard dashed into the bank, with the bad guy in chase.

Little did the robber suspect, police officer Daniel Brister was inside. He wasn't there as protection. He just happened to be there. As the two men ran into the bank, Brister turned toward them. He quick-drew his revolver.

The robber, gun already drawn, was prepared to use it from the beginning. In the ensuing gunfire, Officer Brister fell dead.

The killer ran, escaping. Under the circumstances of the times, there were no police available to give chase.

At present, the Mediterranean Chef occupies the spot where the bank stood in 1920. And yes, the alleged spirit of Daniel Brister is said to haunt the café. The owner tells of one of his waitresses who said she saw the apparition of a policeman in a uniform of those days. Uniforms of the 20s were dark, high-collared, with buttons up the jacket front, and a bright badge on the left.

It is also the case where employees in the past have refused to work the night shift, especially if only one employee was still there just before closing. Plates and other serving pieces moved in front of the owner's eyes. I'll accept that.

Upon reading accounts of this incident two or three times, I thought what an eerie story.

There were very few "armored" cars in use at that time. Only a detail, which doesn't change the fact that a ghost stays around the Mediterranean Chef.

In researching, I learned police departments of any large city would confirm that earlier records of officers killed in the line of duty were easily lost. When my deputy-sheriff grandfather was killed in the line of duty, his name was not in the official records.

Some say they can hear faint gunshots.

Nonetheless, a follow-up of Daniel Brister's death was in the December 20, 1920 (or Fri., Oct. 15) issue of *The Galveston Daily News*.

Just ask if Officer Brister is still around. He said he turns the lights on and off and adjusts electrical equipment at all hours.

Mediterranean Chef
2402 Strand Street
Galveston, Texas 77550
409-765-7700

LUIGI'S RESTORANTE ITALIANO

The professional review is in. "Renowned chef Luigi Ferre turns out spectacular Tuscan-style Italian food at Luigi's Restorante Italiano." People have known that for years. That's not all you will find at Luigi's. There is apparently a woman's spirit who keeps watch over the restaurant.

The catastrophic hurricane of 1900 took thousands of lives and destroyed so much of Galveston, it's no wonder hauntings abound throughout the city. Many storeowners have learned to live with the ghosts. Some employees don't look at it that way and simply quit.

Spirits don't just leave at the turn of another year. Or after the turn of another hurricane.

Dash Beardsley, the "Ghostman of Galveston," knows the story, and Michael Graczyk reported it in the *Victoria Advocate*. A former manager offered his opinion about the ghost he believes inhabits Luigi's Restorante Italiano. Even before he became involved with the restaurant, he had heard it was haunted.

I don't know how he arrived at her identity as Sara, but the story is, during the Great Flood, someone named Sara saved victims by pulling them up the iron stairs to the second floor. She soon died from one of the diseases that struck so many after the hurricane.

The manager didn't particularly believe in the paranormal. Okay, he was a skeptic. But one evening, while he was alone and getting ready to close, he heard a woman's voice calling his name. She called it twice. Of course, he thought someone was still in the restaurant, perhaps a waitress whom he thought had already left. But he found no one.

Even though the voice was not loud, it was clear. Later on, the owner's small grandson told him about the lady upstairs who seemed friendly, and he spoke to her. Since nobody would have been on the second floor, the manager was convinced—that and the fact someone else had told him the image of a woman was in a picture they had taken. She wasn't visible at the time. Hazy photos of people often show up on film when no one can see them with the naked eye.

According to Beardsley, he thinks the woman may have been a victim of the 1900 storm and possibly drowned near the place in which her spirit has appeared. She's dressed in Victorian clothes and he's seen her walk past the windows on the upper floor.

Employees of the restaurant have said they heard footsteps on the stairs and, at other times, whispers when no one was there. Everyone was gratified to learn he hadn't been dreaming. He was no longer a skeptic.

Perhaps Sara will stroll by your table.

If owner/chef, Luigi Ferre isn't too busy in the kitchen, ask him if he would sing—anything to his liking. If he will, I promise, you won't be sorry you asked.

So you can have Grecian for lunch at the Mediterranean Chef (perhaps see the misty lady) and Italian for dinner down the street at Luigi's (and maybe run into Officer Brister.)

That's two ghosts for the price of . . . two.

Luigi's Ristorante Italiano
2328 Strand Street
Galveston, Texas 77550
409-763-6500

THE TROLLEY STATION BUILDING

There are different spirits—different types and time periods. And the Trolley Station Building is home to more than one variety, all apparently "living" in harmony. The building is possibly the most haunted structure in Galveston. Dash Beardsley tells about the ghosts who took up residence on the second floor of this building over 150 years ago. They show no signs of leaving. Then, no one's asked them to.

The 2021 Strand is a long building with several businesses. During the Civil War it held an infirmary and later housed the island's armory. From the street below, people have reported seeing soldiers peer through the windows. One of the stories concerns two Civil War soldiers fighting on Strand Street. When the two turned and fired, the horrendous coincidence was, one was the other's father. He died instantly. Others carried the son to the Trolley Building's infirmary.

Apparitions move across the balcony.

If Civil War soldiers are still trapped there and for some reason can't find the path out, is it because they don't know where the enemy is? Since soldiers from both sides received care in the infirmary, are they still seeking to win the battle in the ghost world, not knowing the battle is already won?

During the 1900 storm, legend tells of the teacher who proved to be a heroine. The water was so high, people were swimming toward any place or thing they could hold on to. When they came close enough, the teacher pulled them through the window. With such swift water, there was nothing she could do as the current snatched them away. The water's force had slung some bodies against the outside wall near the window. The nurse had no idea they were dead until she had drawn them inside.

The balcony area is where the misty images of soldiers sometimes walk. The picture of the inner atrium lobby shows the progress made by my second visit in April 2009. A large portion of the upper floor is also a ballroom, often used for wedding receptions, meetings, and other social events.

Owners of the building have brought back the building to its former self—its nostalgia and beauty—and that surely includes the ghosts of the past.

The Trolley Station Building
2021 Strand Street
Galveston, Texas 77550

BISTRO LECROY

Let's have a look at the ground floor of 2021 Strand. The words here are unexplained shadowy entities. Bistro LeCroy, an upscale seafood restaurant, long-known for its Cajun-style entrees, occupies Suite 3. Not only do people dine there for muffuletta sandwiches, jumbo Gulf shrimp, and crab cakes, they have also heard the restaurant is haunted.

Ghost-hunting film crews and other paranormal investigators have visited the restaurant, hoping to spot a little girl's apparition that wanders in every now and then. Paranormalists have taken seriously what people claimed to have seen in Bistro LeCroy. As a result, their findings have shown a high level of paranormal activity.

Various diners have reported apparitions seemingly floating close to the ceilings. One answer may be they are residual hauntings, a moment in time imprinted in the environment—those victims who floated to the surface in the same building in 1900.

Notice the distinct orb about twelve inches from owner Tomie LeCroy's hand. The wooden post had nine months to dry, so that lets out moisture as the cause for the orb. After Ike struck, silt and mud filled the place from the floor to slippery tabletops, to shelves high above the bar—a similar fate other businesses faced. It isn't always easy to comprehend the fierceness of water.

LeCroy rode out the storm from inside the building. He gazed down from the inner balcony at the big oak-top tables he had built, as they floated in the water. With faith, courage, and probably an aching back, he completely refurbished his business. Water soaked the very special long oak bar, but he took care of that too, and it looks good as new. Not new exactly—after all, it *is* an antique. He brought the tables back to life as well.

Unfortunately, Hurricane Ike destroyed most of LeCroy's paranormal pictures, taken over the years. One in particular was of a human form standing just behind the center post showing the orb.

LeCroy told me that for many years, students and others who live in the apartments across the street, have told him they have seen misty forms

Tomie LeCroy shows the high-water mark of Hurricane Ike. *Courtesy of Barb Gatlin*

walk past the upstairs windows. Some are soldiers and another is a long-haired woman wearing a period dress. As time goes by, a new resident of an apartment will say the same.

The Bistro's inside entrance is just to the left of the Trolley Building's lobby. This part of the building dates to around 1894, although other parts of the building date from three or four earlier decades. But the phantoms have never left. They still gaze down from balconies to the people below. So while you're dining at Bistro LeCroy, relax and propose a toast to a ghost!

Bistro LeCroy
2021 Strand, Ste. #3
Galveston, Texas 77550
409-762-4200

FACE OFF

But it isn't. The "Face" is there to stay, right on Ewing Hall's massive wall at the University of Texas Medical Branch in Galveston. And how did it get there? Although I can't come up with the answer, I can tell you legends surrounding it.

Ewing Hall is the namesake of Maurice Ewing, a UTMB alum. Since the construction of the building in 1972, it is known as one of the most haunted places on Galveston Island. It's reasonable that all sorts of tales surface concerning the immovable "face."

A list of what people believe the source is provides enough theories to help you decide. And if it isn't any of those, what exactly is the source? Keep in mind, there *is* an image on the wall and it *is* a human image.

Conjectures about the mysterious face are: A previous owner of the land lost everything in the 1900 storm and haunts Ewing Hall, because it replaces the space he once owned.

Reportedly, the owner left specific instructions for his offspring not to sell the land until after his death. They sold it to UTMB anyway; therefore, he left his haunting face on the wall.

But the area where Ewing Hall is now was actually in the bay in 1900. Crews hauled in tons of dirt before a building could stand, so underwater land likely wouldn't have sold.

A plausible story is the original owner told his family not to sell the land after he died. He wanted it kept in the family. After his death, they sold the land UTMB now sits on. If that is true, he *does* know how to hold a grudge, and wouldn't let them forget it! It's possible that story developed after Maco Stewart Jr. left instructions in his will for his ranchland, which lay west of his mansion, to be given Texas for the Maco Stewart State Park. This was to happen after all his heirs died, which was estimated to be around 2010.

An additional theory is a homeless man lived on the land, and the contractors bulldozed his shack and what few possessions he had. Therefore, he was a little miffed and stayed around to glare from the wall. And there's the wild thought the face might be that of Jean Lafitte, never wanting to leave the bay where he once led the Phantom Pirates of Barataria.

Back to getting the face off. Or not. If it indeed has control over where it looks, it is very stubborn. To begin with, it's in a corner above the door on the west end of Ewing Hall. You can't miss it.

Unfortunately, at least one tragedy came out of either interest or curiosity. A nurse drove her car around to the west side so she could get a better view. While trying to find an appropriate spot, she backed over into the bay and drowned.

The face is eerie. It stares back with hard eyes. Well, yes, they're concrete. Some say the image is merely an imperfection in the cement. But this is different. We're into paranormal here.

I had seen pictures of the face before, but seeing it for real is *entirely* different.

Since its expression was not that pleasant, UTMB asked the contractor to sandblast it. It didn't work, so he received more money for specialized equipment, which seemed to succeed. But the face returned in a couple days. Frustrated, the maintenance crew waited and tried again, only to see the image reappear. They decided to leave it alone for the time-being.

Fast forward to 1993. The university again tried to have the face removed. Maintenance sandblasted and power-washed it. This time it stayed away two weeks before reappearing, so they dismissed the effort. The face is just there, for all to discuss theories as to why it was there in the first place, and why it can't or can be a real spirit embedded in the wall.

Still, there's something about those eyes. . . .

University of Texas Medical Branch
301 University Blvd.
Galveston, Texas 77555
www.utmb.edu

If we see him, does he see us?

JEAN LAFITTE

There are those who called Jean Lafitte cavalier. Some called him dashing. Those who labeled him clever and corsair were probably nearer the correct description. Don't overlook the label, "Terror of the Seas." Some appreciated his audacity, or were perhaps just in awe.

The son of a Spanish mother and French father, Lafitte was born circa 1776 in? . . . He claimed Bordeaux, France, but Bayonne, Spain, Haiti, and even New York were possibilities. Jack C. Ramsey, Lafitte's biographer, stated that being born in France was more politically helpful for him with his connections in America.

Lafitte was fairly settled in New Orleans by 1805. He stored goods smuggled by his brother, Pierre, in a warehouse in New Orleans. Jean aided his brother in disposing of the merchandise.

While a younger man, he became familiar with every inlet and cove along the Gulf of Mexico. He mapped it out well, obviously planning to use this knowledge in the future. Privateer Lafitte found the area to his liking, enough so, he took over a mansion, which once belonged to Louis-Michel Aury, a French pirate. Boarding houses, pirate huts, saloons and a lucrative slave market occupied the village. With the upper floor converted into a fortress, Lafitte was partly responsible for the extinction of the Karankawas.

He remained there even after Mexico won independence in 1820 from Spain. Concerned after he allegedly attacked an American ship, Lafitte abandoned operations, but not before throwing a party for his pirates. Afterward, he burned his settlement to the ground. A legend formed of Lafitte's having buried his treasure. When such a tale continued through the years, hunters searched in vain for a fortune on this land. In vain then, but will future treasure seekers still arrive with their metal detectors?

On one occasion, a tropical storm caught up with him, and he managed to ride it into Galveston's harbor. He was a master mariner. He and his brothers sailed the Gulf and the Caribbean, bringing their prizes back to Barataria.

Lafitte had either been captured, or surrendered, on more than one occasion and placed into irons. When his personal banker put up bond for him, Lafitte didn't appear for his trial. He was in what he called "The Temple," holding an auction of his plunder.

He succeeded so well in his illegal activities, Governor Claiborne, quite fed up with his antics, issued a proclamation and posted signs throughout the city: "$500 for the capture of Jean Lafitte." A rumor circulated that the governor would give the rogue the death penalty.

A few days later, citizens were greeted by the replacement of Claiborne's posters with those of Lafitte: "$1,500 reward for the capture of Governor Claiborne to be delivered to the island of Barataria. ~ *Jean Lafitte*."

When the governor sent armed soldiers to collect taxes for goods the elegant scoundrel had sold, and they hadn't come back, he felt sure Lafitte's' army had killed them. They eventually returned, bearing gifts, food, and compliments about the "gentleman pirate who had wined and dined them." He was, however, still in trouble with the governor.

Claiborne was not happy with the result, as his orders had come from the U.S. Government. But Lafitte contacted his old friend, John Randolph Grymes, offering him $10,000 to be his emissary. Grymes resigned his job as district attorney the next day, in order to accept Lafitte's case.

Suddenly, actions in that regard halted, as the nation's capital had fallen and the White House burned. English vessels filled the southern coastal waters. The British, wanting a foothold in the Mississippi Valley by taking over New Orleans, pleaded with Lafitte for help. But knowing he had committed so many illegal activities, he was forced to choose sides. He decided to fight on the side of the United States, and did so at the Battle of New Orleans. He thereby hoped to gain a pardon for his misdeeds.

He claimed he never attacked an American ship. Although he was apparently a man without a country, records show he respected our constitution. Lafitte made enough of an impression to have parks and streets named after him, villages and festivals, as well as books written and movies made. Many of us prefer to follow legend over history.

People still search for his buried treasure. But where? In Galveston? Or at Destrehan Plantation, where his spirit walks on moonlit nights? Legend says he buried treasure there. Yet, legend says he also buried treasure on the land of Stewart's Mansion. Lafitte reportedly found several secret hideaways for his gold and jewelry in the network of marshes around Barataria Bay. Others believe all his treasure sank with his ship, *The Pride*, where it went down in the hurricane of 1826.

Consider, Jean Lafitte stands tall in the swamps, with Spanish moss swaying from the trees above. If he waits in the dark as Ed Syers, author of *Ghost Stories of Texas*, suggested, knowing a shadowy boat would slide noiselessly into the watery cove, would there be time?

That sets me to wonder, would there be, in the mysterious force of a brief supernatural moment, time to allow his men to raise the treasure chests from a sunken vessel and guide their boat from the secret cove into the eerie fog?

STEWART'S MANSION

There are at least a dozen haunted mansions on Galveston Island. "At least" can also be more. The Stewart Mansion is one of them.

William Henry Stewart, born in 1818 in Maryland, came to Galveston as a young man. He and his fourth wife, Mary Walker, had three sons and one daughter: Maco (Māso), Minor, Clegg, and Wilamina. Maco founded the Stewart Title Company in 1893. He knew what he wanted to do in the business world, and he accomplished it.

Their son, Maco Jr., at fifty, married Virginia Beall in 1946. Ambitious, he followed in his father's footsteps. He attended Culver Military School, then the University of Texas, where he studied law. In addition, as a wealthy businessman, he was involved in numerous philanthropies and formed the largest title company in Texas.

Stewart's Mansion came to be in 1926 when powerful businessman, George Sealy Jr., built a retreat for himself and his family on the far west end of the island. Even Jean Lafitte was involved in a battle near the property, long before Sealy built the house.

Maco later acquired the mansion as a resort home. The family lived there several years before he sold it, and it again changed hands, always retaining the name, "Stewart's Mansion."

For decades, people have believed the mansion's reputation for being haunted. But haunted by whom? Maco's brothers were also involved with the business and spent time in the resort with him. Any of the family members think of returning?

The years-old legend is Jean Lafitte buried his vast treasure west of the Mansion. Many people have searched. No one has found it—not a single doubloon. Does that mean no treasure is there or just none found?

Stewart willed his ranchland to Galveston for the Galveston Island State Park. The mansion, a Spanish-Colonial Revival style with tiled courtyard, stands vacant at this time on the West End on Stewart Road. At the entry to the property is an arched stone gateway, bearing the inscription, "Stewart's Mansion." The arch flanks a chain-link gate, which opens to the dirt road leading to the mansion. A large stand of oak trees surrounds the house, almost blocking it out—at least in summer. It is also visible through trees from Lake Como. Because of its historic value, the Galveston Historical Foundation will help decide its fate.

A huge painting of pirate Jean Lafitte hangs on the mansion's wall in the great room. He is pictured in dying color—swashbuckler that he is—thrusting his sword forward. Two of his cohorts join him in the mural.

Legend is, the pirates switch places from time to time. It's almost as if they leap off the wall when no one is there . . . and who is to say they don't?

Remember, "No trespassing." And that takes the fun out of going to a haunted place. (The good news is, the great majority of tales in this book welcome you to trespass. Just be sure which ones they are.)

Stewart's Mansion
West End on Stewart Road
Galveston Island, Texas

THE SPIRITS OF GRACE MANOR

Many people think of a haunted house as being old, with briars and overgrowth. But Grace Manor Bed and Breakfast is far from that. A paranormal group recently produced film with definite paranormal images. Their EMF meters spiked, particularly in two bedrooms.

A little history of Grace Manor: John D. Dodson, a British immigrant, arrived in Galveston prior to 1900. W.F. Beers formed the insurance company, Beers, Kenison & Co., with the Kenisons (father and son) as partners. As Dodson was recovering from terrific financial losses from the storm, good fortune came his way, as a fourth partner in the firm. Much of these losses came about when homes for which he had issued loans suffered destruction during the storm. By this time, he had reached the age of thirty-nine and felt assured he could rebuild his finances.

He was quite right, and he commissioned the renowned architect, George B. Stowe, to design a home for him on property he purchased on Galveston's East End. Stowe had designed innumerable mansions on the island, as well as Galveston's orphanage and the depot. Grace Manor, a massive stucco-covered brick house, is possibly one of his masterpieces of the era.

Designed in 1905, Grace Manor reflects the growth and ambition of the island. But could Stowe have thought this impressive structure would welcome a host of ghosts?

In 1942, Thomas Jefferson Holbrook, former Texas state senator, purchased the home.

He lived there a short time, then sold it to a curly-haired Frenchman, John Roubion.

The spectacular Grace Manor. *Courtesy of Barb Gatlin*

Roubion's wife, Lula W., was a madam known for her boarding house on Postoffice Street. One December, the Frenchman invited relatives over for Christmas dinner. He sat at the head of the table in the large, impressive dining room in what is now Grace Manor, with his wife's "working girls" gathered round with family members—a big, happy circle.

Roubion was active in his church and responsible for passing the collection plate. He also received the title of "Mayor of Postoffice Street." After his death in 1988, the house stood vacant for four years. John H. Agee bought the property and restored it as close as possible to its original condition, with hand-painted cherubs on the formal room's domed, blue ceiling.

The current owner envisioned the home as an elegant bed and breakfast and purchased it in 2002. It had always been a residence before Ms. Gatlin, the fifth owner in over 100 years, purchased it and gave it the current name. Her vision became reality. Every square foot is special, as well as the basement—for a different reason. More about the basement later.

Hurricane Ike took away the birds of paradise, hibiscus, and all the other flowers and vines. But with Barb's TLC, you can again look from the balcony outside your room into the gardens below and appreciate the beauty. Evacuating the storm and thinking she'd be back in a couple days, she left her pet kitty behind, with plenty of food in the kitchen. Later, the city would not allow residents to return for several days. When Barb came home, her 19-year-old kitty had disappeared. The city transferred lost pets to Houston for safety until their owners could locate them.

Not all that optimistic, Barb drove to Houston. Something guided her to the right place, because she found her kitty in the back of a cage, looking miffed that it took her mistress so long to come for her. A bit of a miracle—the spirits were in good form that day.

When paranormal investigators visited Grace Manor, they discovered the Island Palm room with high activity. But the Vanilla Orchid room, considered the master bedroom of the house, showed an image of a servant of the 1930s. She was heavy-set, strict of manner, and spoke with a German accent. Others have also seen her image.

Now, back to the basement. When Barb first moved into the manor, she felt a certain peace, as if she had lived there for years. Later on, after listening to comments from guests, who told her of hearing unusual sounds, she contacted a psychic to come to the house. The psychic wanted to go to the basement, a request causing Barb to wince, since it included so many storage items and garden equipment, not allowing for neat perfection.

When they walked down the steps, the psychic insisted on going into one particular section. Barb heard her ask, "Who are you?" She continued to converse with someone named Walter. Of course, Barb heard only the one-sided conversation, but the psychic informed her that a spirit definitely resided in the basement. Even though Barb has not heard anyone speak, when she goes into the basement, she greets the spirit with, "Hi, Walter!"

I didn't mention Barb's breakfast to die for. And if I did, I would hope to have a visitor's guest pass forever. I could even visit Walter. He could tell me all about his world. I'd tell him about my world just before I left it, and urge him to venture upstairs every now and then. In the meantime, consider staying in Grace Manor on your next coastal visit. Barb's loveable golden spaniel, Gracie, will be glad to see you.

Grace Manor
1709 Postoffice Street
Galveston, Texas 77550
409-621-1662
www.gracemanor-galveston.com

ASHTON VILLA

James Moreau Brown, born in 1821, was the youngest of sixteen children. After having an adventurous early life, he eventually left his home in the east, ultimately working his way to Galveston in the 1840s. He went into the hardware business and in his mid-twenties, he was a young man to be reckoned with in the industry.

James Brown married Rebecca Ashton Stoddart Rhodes in 1848. His chosen profession grew, and by the 1850s, he had developed the largest hardware business west of the Mississippi. After amassing a fortune, Brown contacted Samuel Sloan, foremost Philadelphia architect, to design a spectacular brick home. Price was no object in the construction of this dream mansion. Slave laborers and European craftsmen built it according to Brown's specifications. He was a trained mason and if necessary, had no problem supervising.

The Browns named their home Ashton Villa, after Rebecca's father. They owned one of the most impressive houses on the island—$4,000 for the land and $18,000 total. Long vertical windows and ornate verandas topped with cast-iron lintels distinguish this majestic home built in the Victorian Italiante style. Brown insisted interior walls be thirteen inches thick for protection against damp weather along the coast. Kenneth Hafertepe, in *A History of Ashton Villa*, describes the mansion, as well as the elaborate lives, both happy and sad, of the Brown family.

During the Civil War, Ashton Villa served as a hospital for Confederate soldiers. Since at various times either Confederate or Union forces controlled Galveston, Ashton Villa was headquarters for whoever had control. When the war ended, history tells us Confederate forces in the southwest surrendered in the mansion's Gold Room. It's the focal point of the home, lavishly decorated with family heirlooms and original paintings.

The Brown's daughter, the striking and sophisticated Miss Bettie Brown, presided over this magnificent showcase. She grew up privileged among extravagant surroundings. Her free spirit was not unlike those "free spirits" of modern times, depending on our definition. She loved to travel, collect ornate fans, and buy expensive gowns. In other words, she loved to collect things, including male admirers.

Picture this: Galveston, 1865. A palatial, three-story architectural masterpiece, a mansion now in the city's historical district. Now visualize a tall, beautiful, golden-haired woman. Bettie Brown stands on a floral-carpeted stairway—a pose reminiscent of a grand lady of the Victorian age, expecting her guests for tea, or perhaps she is waiting for a gentleman caller.

In those years, closets as we know them today were not the norm; however, the Browns rejected the armoire-type and had a built-in closet in each bedroom. Bettie was sure to have appreciated that, considering her penchant for sumptuous clothes. As for her gentlemen friends, she may have kept a diary, although no one ever found one.

James Brown died in 1895, leaving Ashton Villa to his wife. After her death, their remaining children divided one of the largest fortunes in the state. Miss Bettie Brown, who never married, inherited the house.

During Galveston's 1900 hurricane, Brown's widow, Rebecca, opened the mansion's front and back doors, allowing water to flow through the hall and out the rear. Even with water rising six feet and causing much damage, their plan kept the house on its foundation. One of the younger daughters sat on a high step of the staircase, watching water rush through.

When the flood subsided, workers cleared the house of mud and silt. They moved furniture and objects d'art to higher levels of the house, so perhaps the material loss was not as great as it could have been. After the Browns passed on, time and neglect took its toll on this piece of history.

One of the granddaughters sold the house in 1927 to the El Mina Shrine. Shriners occupied the mansion until 1968 when they offered it for sale. With the threat of Ashton Villa's demolition in view, to be replaced with a filling station, the Galveston Historical Foundation raised $125,000 to purchase and restore this antebellum landmark, which became a museum open to the public in 1974. It serves as the Heritage Visitors Center and is also on the list of the National Register of Historic Places.

Miss Bettie Brown apparently never altogether left her home. Neither flood nor death could dispossess her. People have said they've seen and heard, if not felt, her presence in the elaborate Gold Room. The family returned many of the furnishings to the house, including Miss Brown's collections of art treasures.

A night caretaker awoke during a storm to hear an incessant barking of a dog. The man lived in an outer cottage. He rushed to the main house, thinking someone had broken in. Upon entering, he heard a couple arguing. Of course he had no way of knowing who was there, although he knew no one should have been.

The caretaker entered the large room and viewed a beautiful woman seated at the piano, a handkerchief held to her eyes. As she sobbed, a handsome dark-haired man glanced down at her. They each wore nineteenth-century clothes. Equally cross words accompanied the man's

Miss Betty Brown apparently still calls it home.

cross expression. He told her a man would be foolish to try to talk to her—she had interest only in her good looks and material possessions.

Calling him "Harrison," the woman wouldn't listen to such hateful words and began playing the piano.

The caretaker watched her, but when he returned his gaze to the man, he had vanished. Bettie Brown stood, sobbing as she walked over to a wall mirror. Peering into it, she asked, "Mirror, Mirror on the wall, who is the fairest of all?" She then dissolved into thin air. Fact or fiction? Remember, after a sensitive dog barked wildly, the caretaker witnessed the anomalous scene.

Miss Brown's favorite possessions are on display in the Gold Room, where her presence is strongest. Legend is, her spirit also hovers near the second-floor landing. A guide reported seeing her apparition in that area. Others have had similar experiences there. Dressed in a ravishing gown, she carried an elaborate lace fan from her collection.

Museum tourists have believed someone unseen was with them, as if delighted by their interest in the villa. According to one tourist, the furniture moves around, and clocks stop ticking, but not because they need winding. A chest in Miss Brown's dayroom will lock and unlock itself. The key disappeared years ago.

One most unusual thing is a particular bed that will not stay made. An attendant can straighten it several times a day, and still, the coverlet is rumpled. Is Bettie Brown indulging in brief ghost naps? Her beauty sleep, perhaps.

Remember, if you tour this historical mansion, the stunning Miss Brown may greet you. If she appears to wander off, she may be searching for Harrison. Unfinished business with someone she may have really loved might hold her in Ashton Villa . . . waiting.

The stately mansion is one of a few standing after the great hurricane of 1900—its thick walls showing Mr. Brown's gift for prescience. James Moreau Brown and his family entertained the rich and famous, and now, it is visited by the more or less, rich and famous of today.

September 13, 2008 left the lower floor of Ashton Villa soaked with water. Furniture began molding within days of the hurricane. Workers pulled up the carpet and pad to get to the hardwood floors before they buckled to the point of no repair. The astonishing fact is, a refurbished Ashton Villa re-opened on Thanksgiving, slightly more than two months after Hurricane Ike. It would take a while to replenish the landscaping.

1859 Ashton Villa
2328 Broadway
Galveston, Texas 77550
For Information: 409-762-3933

After the Great Flood of 1900:

> *"Yet the city had a ghostly charm. The scent of tangled gardens hung heavy on the muggy air. The houses . . . seemed built of ashes. Here was a remnant of haunted beauty—gray, shrouded, crumbling."*
> —Edna Ferber, *A Kind of Magic*.

. . . That was then. This is now. The island has risen from the ashes and devastation of Hurricane Ike, and we again experience Galveston's charm.

Conclusion

Everyone, skeptics included, has pondered the possibility of a ghost's existence. Can a person's spirit actually remain on earth?

If we knew for a fact what ghosts were, there might not be so much interest in searching for them. So far, after thousands of years, there is no specific answer. That doesn't stop us from trying to prove or disprove their existence. Since ancient times, all the world's cultures have accepted the supernatural.

No matter the size of the town, or its age, ghosts of the past are surely lurking there. Lurking may sound ominous—it's how we interpret them that causes us alarm.

When visiting any haunted place in this book, above all, hold respect for the dead. If you run into a ghost or two who turn out to be more than a figment of your imagination, remember, they claimed residence first.

So take this haunted tour of Houston, Galveston, and nearby areas—its ghosts await you!

Glossary

Anomaly
Something strange or unusual.

Apparition
A strange or supernatural thing.

Aura
A light surrounding a person, believed to reflect the person's personality.

Banshee
In Irish legend, a wailing sound, which seems to be in more than one place at the same time, announcing an imminent death.

Channeling
When a spirit passes information to a medium, who then relays it to the person who wishes to hear what the spirit has to say to him or her.

Clairvoyant
Seeing beyond normal sight. Sometimes called "second sight."

Demon
Usually thought of as a supernatural evil being.

Doppelganger
An exact spirit double or mirror image of a person who is considered negative.

Earthbound
A ghost or spirit that cannot cross "into the light" and is stranded on earth.

Ectoplasm
A material associated with spirit manifestations. A form of spirit energy, sometimes swirling in photographs.

Electronic Voice Phenomenon (EVP)
Sounds or voices from beyond, recorded on tape.

EMF Detector
Measures the magnitude and direction of a magnetic field. Paranormal investigators use it to detect a ghost's magnetic energy.

Extra Sensory Perception (ESP)
Communication by means other than the physical senses.

Illusion
What is perceived and what is reality.

Levitation
A person or thing rising from a surface in defiance of gravity.

Medium
Someone who professes a talent for communicating with spirits.

Mist
Shows up in a photograph as just that—a mist, often believed to be a spirit.

Orb
Rarely seen by the naked eye. A photographed anomaly in the form of a circle, pale to vivid in color, occasionally with a tail. Some people believe orbs are spirits of deceased, although that is questionable in paranormal identification, since it could be a dust speck or moisture drop.

Paranormal
Beyond the area of scientific explanation or normal human experience.

Parapsychology
Deals with the study of psychic phenomena.

PERCIPIENT
A person who sees, as in perceives, an apparition.

PHANTOM
A form, which is heard, seen, or merely sensed, but has no physical reality. Appearing in the mind.

PRECOGNITION
The ability to perceive something in advance of its occurrence, as in ESP.

PRESCIENCE
The power to foresee the future.

PSYCHIC
A person who is responsive to psychic forces with above average ESP abilities.

REVENANT
Term for ghost.

RESIDUAL HAUNTING
Common type of haunting; a re-run of a past event imprinted onto a specific location for a moment in time, coming from the past. The apparitions are not spirits; they are merely recordings of the event.

SEANCE
A meeting of people, with a medium receiving spiritualistic communication with the dead.

SHADE
Term for ghost.

SPECTER
A ghostly apparition.

SPIRIT
A spirit can manifest itself when it wishes and knows well it has passed on over/up/down.

SPIRITUALISM
The belief that the dead can communicate with the living, via a medium or intermediary.

URBAN LEGEND
A myth and tales handed down for years.

VORTEX
A white rope-like anomaly appearing in a photograph, believed to represent portals to the afterlife. (Be sure your camera strap isn't across the camera lens.)

WILL-O'-THE-WISPS
Wisps are phenomena made of natural gas. They hover over water, swampy or clear. They move fast, causing us to think they are chasing us.

WRAITH
A ghost of a person just before death.

BIBLIOGRAPHY

BOOKS

Abbott, Olyve Hallmark, Ghosts in the Graveyard: Texas Cemetery Tales,   Plano, Texas: Republic of Texas Press, 2001.

_____, "One if by Sea," "Fit for a Queen and King," "A Third Time's a Charm," A Ghost in the Guest Room: Haunted Hotels, B&Bs, and Inns, Dallas, Texas: Atriad Press, 2007.

Allwright, John C., *Fort Bend Ghost Stories*, Richmond, Texas: John C. Allwright, 2000.

_____. *Fort Bend Ghost Stories, Part Two*, Richmond, Texas: John C. Allwright, 2001.

Bellanger, Jeff, *The World's Most Haunted Places*. Franklin Lakes, New Jersey: New Page Books, 2004.

Davis, Camilla Trammell, *Seven Pines*. Dallas, Texas: Southern Methodist University Press, 1986.

Farwell, Lisa, *Haunted Texas Vacations*. Boulder, Colorado: Westcliffe Publishers, 2000.

Foster, Catherine Munson, *Ghosts Along the Brazos*. Waco, Texas: Texian Press, 1977.

Hudnall, Ken, and Sharon Hudnall, *Spirits of the border V: The History of the Lone Star State*. Omega Press, 2005.

McComb, David G., *Galveston A History*. Austin, Texas: University of Texas Press, 2002.

North, Thomas, *Five Years in Texas*. Whitefish, Montana: Kessinger Publishing Company, 2007.

Syers, Edward, *Ghost Stories of Texas*. Waco, Texas: Texian Press, 1981.

MAGAZINES

Block, W. T., "Nicaragua Smith Still Haunts Graveyard." Galveston, Texas: Southwestern Historical Quarterly, Vol. XXI, 1998, No. 4.

Parsons, Jim, "Haunted Houston: Tales of Texas Ghosts and Ghouls that Inhabit the Area." Texas Parks and Wild Life, Oct. 31.
"The Haunting of Liberty County." Liberty, Texas: Outlook Magazine, 10-07.

NEWSPAPERS ONLINE

Graczyk, Michael. "The Haunted Haunts of Galveston." Galveston, Texas: The Associated Press, 10-28-2006.
McDonald, Sara, "What Makes Galveston a Haunted City." Galveston, Texas: The Galveston County Daily News, 10-14-97.
McKay, Paul, "Crime spurs worry in area of Woodlands/Merchants considering tighter security measures." Houston, Texas: Houston Chronicle, 10-07-1996.
Milling, T. J., "Store manager shot to death in The Woodlands." Houston, Texas: Houston Chronicle, 9-22-1996.
_____, "Tip leads to arrest in Walgreen store killing." Houston, Texas: Houston Chronicle, 4-19-97.
_____, "Trial underway in Walgreen store killing." Houston, Texas: Houston Chronicle, 1-28-98.
_____, "Man, 20, gets life in slaying at Conroe-area pharmacy." Houston, Texas: Houston Chronicle. 2-06-98.
Nicholson-Preuss, Mari, "A Jefferson Davis Problem: The 1958 Staphylococcus Aureus Epidemic at Jefferson Davis Hospital." Houston, Texas: Houston Chronicle, 9-03-1958.
Reinhold, Robert, "Galveston: A 19th-Century Island City." Galveston, Texas: New York Times, 10-31-82.
Streuli, Ted, "Storm Coffin Washes Ashore on PEI in 1900?" Galveston, Texas: The Galveston County Daily News, 9-08-03.

ONLINE

www.abclocal.go.com/ktrk/story
www.aliencases.conforums.com
www.audensociety.org
www.avenuecdc.org
www.bizjournals.com
www.click2houston.com
www.columbiahistory.com
www.columbustexas.org
www.crimelibrary.com
www.famoustreesoftexas.tamu.edu
www.farshores.org
www.flagshiphotel.com
www.fogisp.org
www.forttours.com
www.fotojones.com
www.freewebs.com/graveyardwolf
www.galveston.com
www.galvestonhistory.org
www.galvestonhistoricalfoundation.com
www.galvestonnaturetourism.com
www.gatorpress.com
www.geocities.com
www.ghosttoursofgalvestonisland.com
www.glasssteelandstone.com
www.globalsecurity.org
www.gracemanor-galveston.com
www.greenrightnow.com
www.handbookoftexas.com
www.hauntedamericatours.com
www.hauntedhouston.com
www.hauntedotthotel.com
www.houstoncitysearch.com
www.houstonist.com
www.htexas.com
www.ideson.org
www.inter-disciplinary.net
www.jeffcarroll-legendarytexas.com
www.oldtownspringonline.com
www.lonestarspirits.org
www.legendsofamerica.com

www.munsons-of-texas.net
www.mytexasgenealogy.com
www.lldreamspell.com
www.nealwitwer.com
www.remainstobeseen.com
www.saleontexas.com
www.sonofthesouth.com
www.realtraveladventures.com
www.unexplained-mysteries.com
www.texasescapes.com
www.Texasexplorer.com/opera
www.texascourthouses.com
www.texaslesstraveled.com
www.texasghosthunters.com
www.theblackvault.com
www.thedailycouger.com
www.thegrand.com
www.theStrand/Galveston.com
www.tpwd.state.ts.us.com
www.tshaonline.org
www.tsl.state.Texas.us.com
www.ustcauldron.org
www.victoriaadvocate.com
www.visithoustontexas.com
www.waymarking.com
www.wikipedia.com
www.wtblock.com
www.wunschebroscafe.com